Amidst the Shadows of Trees

D0768686

Center Point
Large Print

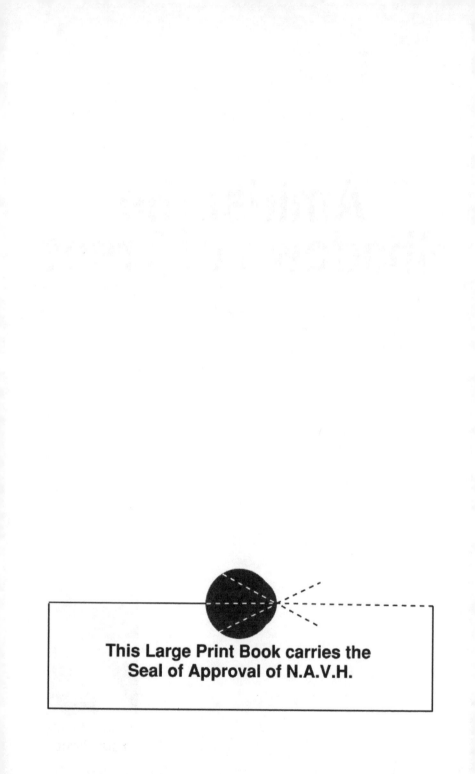

**This Large Print Book carries the
Seal of Approval of N.A.V.H.**

Amidst the Shadows of Trees

A HOLOCAUST CHILD'S SURVIVAL IN THE PARTISANS

Miriam M. Brysk

Introduction by Michael Berenbaum

CENTER POINT LARGE PRINT
THORNDIKE, MAINE

This Center Point Large Print edition
is published in the year 2014 by arrangement with
Gihon River Press.

The text of this Large Print edition is unabridged.
In other aspects, this book may vary
from the original edition.
Printed in the United States of America
on permanent paper.
Set in 16-point Times New Roman type.

ISBN: 978-1-62899-135-2

Library of Congress Cataloging-in-Publication Data

Brysk, Miriam M., author.
Amidst the Shadows of Trees : a Holocaust child's survival in the
Partisans / Miriam M. Brysk ; introduction by Michael Berenbaum.
p. cm.
Summary: "A Holocaust child-survivor shares her memories of
escaping from Lida Ghetto in Belarus with her parents and joining the
Partisans in the Lipiczany Forest as part of the Jewish Resistance"
—Provided by publisher.
ISBN 978-1-62899-135-2 (library binding : alk. paper)
1. Brysk, Miriam M. 2. Holocaust, Jewish (1939–1945)—Belarus—
   Lida—Personal narrative. 3. Jewish children in the Holocaust—
   Belarus—Biography. 4. Jews—Poland—Biography.
   5. Jews—Belarus—Biography. 6. World War, 1939–1945—Jewish
   resistance—Belarus—Biography. 7. World War, 1939–1945—
   Underground movements—Belarus—Biography.
   8. Guerrillas—Belarus—Biography.
   9. Holocaust survivors—Biography. I. Title.
DS134.B383B79 2014
940.53´18092—dc23
[B]

2014012971

IN MEMORY OF MY GRANDPARENTS,
PARENTS AND AUNT ALA

And to my husband Henry,
daughters Judy and Havi

and grandchildren Benjamin, Joshua, David,
Sarah and Hannah

CONTENTS

PREFACE

In the summer of 1989, I accompanied my husband on a business trip to Paris. While exploring the city on my own, I wandered into an old neighborhood of very narrow cobblestone streets. Deep in the shadows, attached to the wall of a building, I noticed a plaque written in *Yiddish*.[1] It was one of several historical markers that identified sites where some of the Jews of Paris were assembled for deportation. As I read it, my vision blurred, and tears began to swell. Feeling overwhelmed with emotion, I sat down on the sidewalk and closed my eyes. I could hear and feel the anguished Yiddish voices of those Jews as their bodies shook in fear and panic. I thought back to my own childhood in the Lida Ghetto after the Nazis invaded the Soviet Union in 1941. I remembered my own family members who had been deported from Warsaw to Treblinka—never to return again . . .

In November 1942, when I was nearly eight years old, Jewish partisans from the Orliansky Group of the Lipiczany Forest rescued us from

---

[1]Related to German, Yiddish is the language spoken by Jews in central and eastern Europe.

the Lida ghetto; they wanted to bring my father to the forest to operate on wounded Russian partisans. A month after we came to the forest, German soldiers mounted an attack in our forest in an attempt to kill partisans and Jews. As the partisans scattered in different directions throughout the forest, they abandoned us because they were afraid of having a child along who might cry out in fear and alert the enemy on their whereabouts. My mother and I wandered in the forest without food or water, and nearly froze to death. After the Germans left, we were reunited with my father. In time, a forest hospital was established with my father as chief of staff. Because many single women were raped by the Russian partisans, my father wanted to protect me by turning me into a boy. He shaved my head and my mother sewed boys clothing for me to wear. On my eighth birthday, I was given a pistol of my own which I proudly wore on my side. I was taught how to use the gun but never wounded or killed anyone. After a year and a half in the partisans surviving many more German attacks, we were liberated when Russian tanks entered the forest in the early summer of 1944.

After liberation, we lived in the nearby town of Szczuczyn for a few months where my father was put in charge of the municipal hospital. The Communist authorities then awarded my father the Orden Lenina (Order of Lenin), one of the highest Russian medals, for his medical contributions in the partisans. Nonetheless, we realized more and more that we did not want to live under Communism. Later that year, things came to a head when new orders from Moscow banned travel by essential personnel such as doctors. We fled surreptitiously from Szczuczyn to Lublin in Poland. From there we traversed all of Central Europe as part of the great postwar European movement of displaced refugees, until we came to the United States in February of 1947. And while we were able to create new lives in America, the memories of our old lives in Europe and the loss of our families never left us.

My strong reaction to the plaque remembering the plight of Parisian Jews made it clear that I needed to document my own story about life as a child in the Holocaust. I would focus on my experiences and emotions as a child living in the Lida ghetto and with the partisans in the forest. And I would include details of Jewish Resistance that have not been documented—especially the actions of Jews rescuing other Jews. My intent was to write an honest, accurate and detailed account of my experiences during the Holocaust— reflecting the values by which I live. I hope that my book will add to the undeniable evidence that refutes the efforts of those who continue to deny the Holocaust.

• • •

The Holocaust that destroyed six million Jews also destroyed the rich Yiddish traditions of hundreds of years of Jewish life in Europe. It killed my grandparents, and nearly killed my parents and me. For many years after the war, I kept asking myself why had I survived, why had I been spared? What was my mission in life? How could I honor those who had been lost? Over the last few years, however, I have come to realize that it is more important to live life fully than to question it. I have tried to experience life in all its pain and all its glory, and to live it in a spirit of faith and trust. The best tribute I can give to the memory of those who perished in the Holocaust is to live the kind of life that they themselves would have wanted to live.

Every Survivor has a unique story to relate, a new vantage point for imparting the events of the past. This is my story. Six million such life stories will never be told.

MIRIAM BRYSK
Ann Arbor, Michigan
2013

ACKNOWLEDGMENTS

It took many years to write *Amidst the Shadows of Trees*. The demands of a career in academia, the illnesses and deaths of my parents and the transition into retirement always seemed to take precedence over writing about my life's experiences. In 2000, however, when I retired, I had at last attained the physical and emotional space to devote to this project. I am deeply grateful to Margaret McAnulty, my psychiatric social worker for many years, who has helped me free myself from depression and allowed me to lead a self-assured and creative life.

My first trip back to Poland and Lithuania in 2002, to view the remains of the ghettos, camps and killing sites of the Holocaust, so stirred up memories of my own experiences that I immediately returned to writing my book. With its completion in 2007, came a new challenge: how to get it published. Worried about my longevity, I opted to self-publish while I searched for a publisher. It wasn't until the end of 2012 that I was introduced to Stephen Feuer, the extraordinary publisher of Gihon River Press. He is committed to producing quality books that memorialize the Holocaust. I am grateful that he was interested in publishing my memoir. He has made a dream come true for me.

I thank Sidney Bolkosky and Kenneth Waltzer for their comments about the importance of my story in telling the history of Partisan Resistance in my forest. I also want to acknowledge Barbara Werden for her layout work on this book.

I am extremely grateful to Joanne Gilbert, the woman who became my editor. I am awed by her grasp of Holocaust history, as well as her editorial skills. Her careful and precise edits greatly improved my book. She herself is now writing a book: *Women of Valor: Female Resistance to the Nazis*, to be published by Gihon River Press. That book is based on her first-hand interviews with Jewish and Gentile women who had been in Resistance movements in Poland, France and Holland, and survived into their 90s.

I am deeply honored by Michael Berenbaum's introduction. His words put the Holocaust into perspective as the aging Survivors are losing their battle with time. He captures the uniqueness of my story and endorses its publication.

I am most grateful to my husband Henry and our daughters, Judy and Havi, for their continuous love and support.

MIRIAM BRYSK
Ann Arbor, Michigan
2013

INTRODUCTION

Soon, all too soon, the last Holocaust Survivor will be no longer. Generally, most Survivors of the Holocaust were between the ages of 18 and 40. Sixty-eight years after the end of World War II and the liberation of the camps, the forty-year-olds have gone to their eternal rest, and the eighteen-year-olds are now in their mid-eighties. But even those who escaped death then—even those who routed the devils of death bent on their destruction—cannot defeat the Angel of Death now at the end of a long life.

Survivors offer us unique entry into the world of the Holocaust. Some of us may learn the history the *Shoah*, as well as its sociological origins, the psychology of its perpetrators, the political mechanisms by which the Nazis seized and maintained power, and the ways the Jews responded to their desperate plight. We cannot, however, understand what it was like to be there, unless we heed the testimony of those who were there. As Primo Levi warned us, we say "hunger" and it means we missed a meal or we say "cold" and it means we need a jacket. Those who lived through those times use the same words but it means so much more.

The last of the Survivors will be those who were

very young when they went through the events and who saw them through a child's eye. Because they were so very young, they will remain with us just a bit longer. For many years their testimony was dismissed as insignificant. After all, what could a child know, what could they remember? For years, children-survivors insisted that they had a story to tell, if only we were ready to listen—and if only older Survivors would not dismiss their testimony as insignificant and their memories as distorted.

Shortly after her arrival in America, Miriam Brysk was told that her memories were insignificant; they would fade. She recounts the "helpful" comments she received:

> "How lucky you are to have gone through the world as a child."
> "Only an adult could fully understand what was going on during the war."
> "You were too young to know what was really happening."
> "You will soon forget the past: we don't want you to dwell on the war; remember you are now in America."

And to our benefit, she has now, at last, refused that "sage" advice.

We must welcome Miriam Brysk's memoir, *Amidst the Shadows of Trees: A Holocaust Child's Survival in the Partisans*, for its rare glimpse into the life of partisans, of those men—and so very few children—who fled to the woods to escape not only for their own survival, but more importantly, to fight the German enemy. With the exception of the famed family camps, such as the Bielski Brigade, or the Atlas, Dworecki and Kaplinski Otriads in the Lipiczany Forest, child partisans were very rare indeed.

Fighting units had one mission and one mission alone: to fight unto death, so typical partisan units were composed of young, able-bodied men. Some women could be useful for their companionship and the comfort of their bodies; they were often considered the rewards of fighting men. Most women, however, were deemed an unnecessary hindrance, a drain on the unit's food and medical resources, and a liability in combat. Those who were allowed to stay usually had a man to protect them.

Children were a nuisance, additional mouths to feed, slowing down the fighting unit and hampering their progress. The younger the child, the more precarious they made the situation of the fighting unit. The Bielski group, unlike others, accepted a double mission: to fight the Germans *and* to save Jewish lives. So despite the added risks, they accepted the young and the old, women and children.

Miriam was the exceptional child. Because her father, Dr. Chaim Miasnik, was a surgeon, a good surgeon, a valued and rare medical professional so desperately needed to deal with the wounds of the fighters, he could dictate his terms for joining the partisans, forcing the reluctant fighters not only to accept him, but also his wife and young daughter, Mirele.

Permit me a personal word: my youngest daughter is named Mira and we too call her Mirele, so every time "Mirele" is mentioned in the book, I thought of my daughter and her vulnerabilities. I also thought of Miriam's father's admonition to her mother: "We are alive because we are disciplined. Don't ever forget it." Throughout their four-year ordeal, survival was a matter of luck, skill and discipline. Anything less and they were gone.

Because Miriam was young, readers of all ages will be able to understand her Americanization: the manner in which she not only adjusted to life in post-war America as the child of immigrants, but also the always-present hidden subtext of the life that she had endured. In classrooms throughout Brooklyn and the Bronx in the late 1940s and early 1950s, one could find these children with a hidden, unspoken past. On the surface, Miriam was more fortunate than some. Her parents were still alive, and her highly skilled father could work in his profession. Under the surface, however, she bore the scars of her past.

Miriam writes in a demystified way of her parents, admiring her father's skill and piety—yet understanding only now as an adult, the long-term impact of his harshness toward her. She also sees her mother not in a romanticized way, but as a real woman, going through horrors of her own.

What I specifically appreciate is Miriam's insistence on remaining faithful to her experience. She maintains a child's perspective on those events she experienced as a child. She is more descriptive than analytic and her aspirations are appropriately modest: to tell the reader what she experienced, not to write a history of the partisan movement or an analysis of resistance. Her insights are simple and powerful, yet not simplistic. After writing of the brutal cold of winter in the forests, one expects relief as summer approaches. No such luck as Mirele describes ravenous mosquitoes whose breeding ground is the swamps.

She gives us some important religious insights. Her parents fasted on *Yom Kippur*, even in the forest, even when fasting for days was routine as Jews had nothing to eat. She recounts her father chanting *Kol Nidre* with its haunting melodies. One woman refused to eat anything non-Kosher, even though when one's life was at risk, a religious Jew is permitted to eat non-Kosher. Miriam captures the ambivalent attitude of survivors to religious life immediately after Liberation:

"It was an unbelievably moving experience to witness the refugee Jews huddled together praying to a God we thought had abandoned us. Some were bitter at God for condoning senseless killings. Others refused to believe in God. Where was God's compassion in Treblinka. Many participated only in remembrance of their families who died *oyf Kiddush Hashem* (for the sanctification of His Name). Many were simply grateful to have survived."

Pregnant women had abortions and even pre-pubescent girls were at risk. So Mirele had her hair shaved and went through her partisan years as a boy. She offers us important insights into the rules of survival and the role of women in the partisan units:

"A woman who lived with a permanent man (husband, lover or boyfriend) was spared from overt advances or rape by other men. The unattached woman was fair game for every man and was thus extremely vulnerable. This led to many pairings of women with single men, in order to keep the women safe."

I recall that many years ago at one of the first child survivors' conferences, a then middle-aged man asked if anyone else had gone through the war years as a girl. Reticently, several adult men raised their hand. It was dangerous to hide as a boy for circumcision could reveal that you were a Jew. In the woods, it was dangerous to be a girl, even a young girl.

The older Miriam grows throughout the book, the more willing she is to add to the narrative the insights born of age and distance, the understanding she gained through her hard won psychological work on herself. She is candid with the reader, and as I suspect, is quite candid with herself as well. Her parents did not get along well with each other and her father's demands frightened her. She felt abused, intimidated and disrespected.

We gain the wisdom of a woman who now in her seventies, is able to not only reflect back on her entire life, but generously shares her insights with her readers. Miriam's accomplishments were—and continue to be—many. She married, raised a family, pursued and achieved her doctorate, gained significant professional respect as a scientist, a writer and an artist. As we all know, however, we bring our childhood with us even into old age. The shadows remain even as the trees blossom . . . even for one who found shelter in the forest.

MICHAEL BERENBAUM
American Jewish University
Los Angeles, California
2013

Amidst the
Shadows of Trees

SILENT TREES

Horizons of ancient virgin forests
Secure in their rootedness and innocence
Branches of birches and pines
Intertwining their verdant foliage
Nature's living creatures
Aglow with the spark of their creator
The stillness of the night sky
Interrupted by the grasshoppers' song
Dazzling sunbeams of the morning
Momentarily shadowed by soaring birds
For a moment in time long ago
The trees turned black and gray
The resin and sap from their veins
Exuded silent bloody tears
Bystanders at Babi Yar and Ponar
Also there in my town of Lida
Our ghetto assembled at dawn
Its Jews slaughtered by nightfall
Trees bearing silent eyewitness
To carnage and death
Innocent bystanders
To a moment in history
Seeing parents and children
Mercilessly shot and slaughtered
In pits already full with corpses
Dismembered innocent beings

Sacrificed as scapegoats of history
The stench of rotting bodies
Reaching to the very heavens
Beliefs and ideals of an ancient people
Decomposing into eternal extinction
At that very moment
Humanity ceased to exist
Divinity was excommunicated
And life had lost all its meaning
It was a time in history
Of Holocausts and of horrors
Many years have come and gone since
    then
As I attempt to view my past anew
I try in retrospect to still decipher why
I was spared to live while other children
    died
Ev'ry spring the trees again do blossom
Ev'ry year my own children bloom
New saplings from the trees appear
Grandchildren born to me those years
Together they and I live out our lives
Perplexed bearers of a paradoxical legacy

Miriam Brysk
1990

CHAPTER 1

My Family

On September 1, 1939, the Nazis invaded Poland and began to bomb Warsaw, where I lived with my family. Events in the city unfolded more rapidly than a four-year-old child could possibly comprehend. I was terrified as I clung to my mother and Aunt Ala. Nervously looking out the window, I trembled at the sounds of bombs exploding and scenes of houses burning all around us. Ala surveyed the situation, and then closed the shutters so as not to alarm me further. While afraid herself, she was careful not to panic. She tried to impress on me that she was in control, and that everything would be alright.

I stood by helplessly in our apartment at 41 Zelazna Street while Mama hurriedly packed some food while Aunt Ala did the same with our clothing. Mama told me to follow her down the several flights of stairs to our building's front door, and out to the street. As we ran for the nearest shelter, I could see men and women running in panic as low-flying German planes machine-gunned people on the streets. Many also dodged bricks and debris that fell from houses and buildings that were hit by exploding bombs.

Shaking in fear, I kept asking my mother why all this was happening. "You wouldn't understand, Mirele," she tersely replied.

"You must hold on to me at all times," my mother directed. "We must not be separated. You must obey all the orders I give you without asking any questions. Do what I tell you." At that point, I was too scared to cry. My Aunt Ala, sensing my fright, put her arm around me as we took refuge in a designated shelter of a nearby apartment building. The bombing had disrupted the electricity, and the basement was so dark that we could barely see each other's faces. As we huddled together in a corner, I asked, "Where are Grandma and Grandpa? Are they safe?" Ala assured me that they were safe in a shelter similar to ours on Sienna Street, where they lived.

Then I asked about Papa and my uncles. Ala responded that they were safe too, but did not tell me that they had already left Warsaw. After the Germans attacked Poland, the Russians urged able-bodied men to cross over into the Soviet-occupied area of Poland. As a result, my father and my uncles left Warsaw and headed for my father's home town of Lida in Belorussia. We agreed that after Warsaw fell, we would cross over the border and join our family in Lida. Since Ala had always been my "other" mother, her answers satisfied me and, cradled in her arms, I again felt safe. More than anyone, she knew how to calm me and make me feel secure. As her soft, loving voice resonated inside me, I smiled and closed my eyes.

In contrast to the chaos in the streets, the people in the shelter were quietly praying that we would not sustain a direct hit. Suddenly, a bomb whistled overhead and entered our building—everyone held their breath—but the bomb did not explode. After the all-clear signal, others found the bomb in a nearby bathtub that had been filled with water for drinking. The water had apparently prevented it from detonating. This was the first of many bombardments that marked the invasion of Poland. In the ones that followed, we hid along with my grandparents.

My maternal grandparents, Ita (Zemelman) and Avram Zablocki, were observant Jews and respected members of the Twarda Street Synagogue. They owned a restaurant at 17 Zielna Street, providing the family a good income. Together they had five children: Henry, Morris, Bronka, Sevek, and Ala. Bronka, born on January 23, 1909, became my mother. *Shabbos*,[2] when the restaurant was closed, was the only day they could all be together as a family. In this busy environment, the children became independent while still very young.

The older boys helped raise their younger

_____

[2]*Shabbos*, also known as the Sabbath, is observed by religious Jews as the biblical day of rest.

siblings and were very protective of them. When they were both barely twenty, Henry and Morris left for America to avoid serving in the Polish army. With the departure of her older brothers, Bronka became the senior child in the family. Sevek was very handsome and had a harem of girlfriends who relentlessly pursued him. Bronka let him know that she did not approve of his loose behavior and lack of discipline. At twenty, Sevek was drafted into the Polish army, and he finally was on his own.

Bronka was her father's favorite and could influence him to go along with most of her wishes. She not only got her own desires met, but she often interceded with her father, either for or against the wishes of the other children. She was an assertive young woman, and she soon became the manager of the entire household. Bronka loved her baby sister, Ala, dearly and helped raise her. Unlike Bronka, Ala was the gentlest of all the children. Like her mother, she was quiet and subdued. Although her mother's favorite, she did not abuse her position in the family. Ala, because she was lovable and sweet to all her siblings, did not compete with any of them; in fact, she helped unify the family. Ala was close to her big sister, but as they got older, despite being pretty, her lack of social flair made her uncomfortable keeping up with Bronka's social life.

As was customary in Warsaw, Jewish girls did

not obtain a religious education, so Bronka and Ala never attended religious school. In those days, girls were expected to be married by age twenty, at the latest. After finishing *gymnasium* (high school), they worked for local Jewish merchants. Bronka, an elegant young woman with short brown hair, deep green eyes, and a small pug nose, loved to dress up and go to dances and parties. While she was popular with young men, she did not meet anyone with whom she had a serious relationship. Her concerned parents and brothers made an effort to introduce her to suitable men to marry. When she was twenty-three, however, she met a young Jewish doctor from Lida who was finishing his surgical residency in Warsaw.

Although Dr. Chaim Miasnik was neither handsome nor tall, he was a brilliant doctor. He came from a small town and lacked the sophistication of big city life, and sometimes was socially awkward. When he met Bronka, he instantly fell in love with her, calling her his "Broneczka." Obsessed with her, he stole a picture of her from her parents' house! While it was not love at first sight for Bronka, her family con-vinced her that it was a good match. The couple married on September 10, 1933. She would be his beloved for the rest of their chaotic lives. But the marriage was troubled. Chaim worked around the clock, and Bronka was disappointed and angry over their lack of a social life. Most disturbing was his fiery temper, which flared at the least provocation, and there were constant arguments between them. She would stop talking to him for days until he apologized—a response that incensed him even more. In the end, however, he always caved in. Bronka began to feel trapped in her marriage but became resigned to live with this man even though he often did not understand her or her needs. Great joy came to them two years later, however, when Bronka gave birth to their first child, daughter Mirele. It was midnight, the beginning of a new day, March 10, 1935.

"Congratulations, Pani Doctorowa (Mrs. Doctor's Wife) Miasnik," Bronka was told. "You just gave birth to a little girl. You gave birth so quickly that you almost had her on the way to the hospital! With such an easy birth, we should be seeing you every year." So reassured, Bronka held her child in her arms, fondly touching her baby's little fingers, and examining all the body parts of her bald-headed little daughter. As her maternal instincts surged, she smiled with great pride and satisfaction.

Chaim had hoped for a son who would follow in his footsteps, but there was time to have other children, including a son. Their thoughts now turned to naming their daughter. Since it is a Jewish custom to name newborns in honor of dead relatives, Bronka and Chaim reviewed the list of such relatives. It appeared, however, that those names had already been used several times over. It seemed appropriate to give their daughter a new name, one that she alone would define in her own lifetime. So they named me Mirjam (Mirka). As a child, I would be affectionately called *Mirele* (pronounced mee'-reh-leh) in Yiddish or *Mireczka* in Polish.

My maternal grandparents in Warsaw were overjoyed. My name became a magic word for them. They signed all the letters going to America with the phrase "*mit Mirele b'rosh*" ("with Mirele at the top"), indicating the importance that I played in the family. My uncles in America were immediately notified of my birth. The rest of the family received me with equal excitement. We lived near my grandparents, and on Friday evenings, we went to their home for dinner. My grandfather Avram would hold me on his lap, and while I sat there, I'd make a mess of the food on his plate. He would comment that this made his food taste all the better.

My parents' childhoods were very different. My paternal grandparents, Chana Liba Popko and Chenoch Miasnik, were married in the late 1800s. They lived in a house in a narrow passageway off of Reins Street in Lida. This small city wound up in the newly independent Poland in the aftermath of World War I. When the Germans and the Russians invaded and divided up Poland, it was annexed to Belorussia[3] (in which it has remained). Chenoch was a tall and handsome man, hard-working and quiet. He owned a kosher butcher shop that provided the family with a reasonable income. They had four sons: the eldest, Mordechai, later studied medicine and lived in Warsaw. Two other sons, Chatskel and Broine became butchers and later emigrated from Poland to America. Their smallest and middle son, Chaim (Noach) Miasnik, born in 1903, became my father.

Since Yiddish was the mother tongue of the Jews of Eastern Europe, it was the first language the boys were taught. As they grew, they also became fluent in Polish and Russian. In those days, a public school education was all but forbidden to Jews, so the boys attended a Jewish religious school called a *Cheder*, where they learned Hebrew and the written and oral traditions of Judaism. They learned both biblical and modern Jewish history spanning from the prophets to the sages, from the martyrs to the mystics. They read the stories of Sholem Aleichem[4] and I. L. Peretz[5] in Yiddish, and the poetry of Chaim

---

[3]Belorussia was a component "republic" of the Soviet Union; it is now the independent nation of Belarus.
[4]Sholem Aleichem (1859–1916) was a leading Yiddish author and playwright whose short stories became the basis of *Fiddler on the Roof*.
[5]I. L. Peretz (1852–1915) was a renowned Yiddish poet who advocated for human rights.

Bialik[6] in Hebrew. The Lida religious school also taught secular subjects (science, mathematics, geography, and history) in order to prepare Jewish boys to make a living in a hostile and anti-Semitic Christian world.

The boys helped run the household and butcher shop. On Fridays, the house was meticulously cleaned to welcome the Sabbath. Chenoch brought fresh meat from his butcher shop; vegetables were grown or purchased at the local market, and a *challah*[7] was baked at home. A stew of meat, vegetables, beans, and potatoes called *cholent* was placed in the oven at a low temperature and left unattended to cook overnight, ready to eat at midday after morning worship services. Chenoch recited the *Kiddush*,[8] and all the appropriate blessings were said before the evening meal. The house acquired that special spirit of holiness commanded since biblical times for this day of rest. Judaism is a faith that celebrates the holiness of time.

Chana Liba had her own unique duties to perform. On Fridays, she put on her best clothes

---

[6]Chiam Bialik (1873–1934) wrote in Hebrew and Yiddish, and came to be known as Israel's national poet.

[7]*Challah* is the traditional egg bread baked for the Sabbath.

[8]*Kiddush* is the traditional prayer chanted on the eve of the Sabbath and other Jewish holidays.

and quietly went to call on the more prosperous Jewish merchants in town. Lida was an industrial town with several factories owned and run by Jews; many fine Jewish craftsmen lived and worked there. The majority of the Jews, however, were extremely poor and barely eked out a living. On seeing Chana Liba, the merchants inquired:

"Who needs our help, Chana Liba?"
"How much do you need today?"
"On whose behalf are you here today?"

Many of Lida's poor Jews turned to Chana Liba, their unofficial representative, for help. Her mission—collecting from the merchants—completed, she stopped along the way home to invite poor Jewish street beggars for a Sabbath meal. Food was stretched, as needed, to feed everyone. As a descendent of *Tzaddikim*,[9] Chana Liba lived the traditions of Jewish mysticism that joyfully celebrated the spirit and the essence of the holy covenant between man and God. Judaism was for her a means of serving God through the *menschlichkeit*[10] of man.

Chaim, short like his mother, was born with a severe curvature of the spine. To compensate for

---

[9]*Tzaddikim* is the Hebrew name for Righteous Jews.
[10]*Menschlichkeit* refers to the qualities of a person who exhibits integrity and honor.

his small stature and handicap, he performed many physically demanding tasks in order to build up his muscles and increase his stamina. In time, he acquired the bulging physique and superior strength characteristic of a body builder. Since he was also an avid reader, he would take a break from chopping wood in the forest, to sit under a tree and read the poems of Bialik. They stirred up deep emotions within him, and as he read them he cried. Bialik described the misery and poverty of the Jews in Eastern Europe, including the *pogroms*[11] inflicted on them by Russian *Cossacks*[12] and neighboring Slavs, who blamed the Jews for killing Christ. In Chaim's favorite poem, "To a Bird," Bialik envisioned a bird flying all the way to the ancient homeland of Eretz Israel. He was projecting a time when Jews would be free in a land of their own.

Chaim joined a *Zionist*[13] youth group and began dreaming of immigrating as a pioneer to a future Jewish homeland. He studied diligently and excelled in all his subjects. When he reached manhood at the age of thirteen, his mother

---

[11]*Pogroms* were violent anti-Jewish mob attacks that were supported by the government.
[12]*Cossacks* were trained warriors, who often came on horseback from the hills to attack Jewish villages.
[13]*Zionism* is a form of Jewish nationalism that supports Israel as a Jewish state.

informed him that his days at the religious school were over and that he needed to acquire a trade in order to make a living. She used this occasion to stress the importance of becoming self-sufficient and earning the respect that comes with a good reputation.

"To be a Rabbi requires you be supported by handouts from the community. The rabbinate is not for you, my son," she told him. "Either become an apprentice and learn a trade, or go to school and acquire a profession. I gave you your first name; your last name you will have to earn yourself." Chaim chose the more difficult alternative and applied to the municipal Karol Chodkiewicz Gymnasium, the public high school that rarely accepted Jews. He had to pass examinations which were made even more difficult for Jews. His superior scores, as well as his tireless perseverance, finally paid off, and he was admitted. Such obstacles did not end with the passing of the examinations. School bullies ridiculed and harassed him, calling him an "ugly Jew." They underestimated both his strength and his volatile temper, as he struck back with power and fury. In time they began to respect him. In fact, one of these bullies eventually became his friend, and Chaim tutored him.

Chaim sought to pursue a career in engineering. At that time, however, since engineering schools did not admit Jews, his father suggested he become a physician instead. So he applied to the Stefan Batery Medical School in Vilna, which had previously accepted only a few Jews. At first he was rejected. A kindly Jewish professor at the school intervened on his behalf, however, and he was finally admitted. Elated with his success, he returned home, only to find his beloved father had died of a heart attack. Chaim was heartbroken to lose his father, who was only in his forties.

Decisions had to be made as to how the family could sustain itself and who would run the butcher shop. Because his two brothers had previously immigrated to America, no one was left to run the business. Chaim volunteered to assume the responsibility, but his mother firmly refused. The business was eventually sold. But who would help pay for his tuition and living expenses? Having no savings, the lack of a steady family income was a continuing problem. Chaim would have to look for part-time jobs to pay his way. With a heart sad from having lost his father and leaving his widowed mother, he returned to medical school in Vilna.

Chaim rented a small room in a poor Jewish neighborhood. This expenditure left him with barely enough money to live on; some days he could not afford to buy food other than bread. When he didn't have enough money for trolley fare to school, he walked. He excelled in all his subjects, particularly anatomy. He earned money from his professors by preparing anatomical specimens for classes. He was also secretly paid for completing the required anatomical projects for the rich medical students, many of whom found these menial tasks beneath their dignity.

Chaim worked hard and graduated medical school in 1931. His interest in anatomy led to his decision to pursue a career in surgery. He was accepted for a residency in Warsaw in the surgical hospital directed by the respected Dr. Miszurski. Though he was still very poor, his spirit soared at the prospect of training with a man of Dr. Miszurski's renown, who also happened to be a Jew. During the first two weeks, Chaim was given the task of rolling bandages. Although he did not much like this assignment or understand its purpose, he carried it out with a sense of dignity. At the end of this initiation period, Dr. Miszurski informed the new Dr. Miasnik that the assignment was intended as a lesson in humility and that he had passed it well.

After this unorthodox beginning, Dr. Miasnik went on to become one of the top gastric surgeons in Warsaw, with an office that adjoined our apartment on Zelazna Street. Surgery would remain his greatest passion in life. He excelled as a diagnostician, making accurate assessments from simple physical examinations. In addition to his heavy load of paying patients, he also operated on many poor Jews who could not afford his services. For this dedication he was referred to as "the king of the poor" by those that he helped. Through the years whenever asked, he claimed to have inherited his healing hands from his mother, Chana Liba.

When I was born, Chana Liba came from Lida to stay with us awhile so she could see her granddaughter Mirele for herself. She had never met her other grandchildren, who lived in America. She cared for me deeply, and I adored her. I remember that my grandmother wore dresses with very wide skirts. In her pockets she hid chocolates, meant for me to find and eat. She read to me Jewish folk tales and sang to me Yiddish folk songs. We also shared little secrets. Having had only sons, she enjoyed spoiling a little granddaughter. Papa worked long hours and I did not see much of him. When he was home, my parents quarreled a lot. Ironically, most of the arguments were over money. Papa was still living in the past, not knowing where his next meal would come from. My mother, on the other hand, was always composed and in control, and she never yelled back. It was difficult for my mother's parents to deal with Papa's hot temper. And when Chana Liba visited, even she sternly reprimanded her son for his behavior. She would not tolerate his outbursts, and he instantly cooled off.

Of all my relatives, I was closest to my Aunt Ala, who lived nearby. She hugged and kissed me often, took me for long walks, and played with me in the park. She was fun to be with, and we laughed over the most trivial things. I could confide in her and tell her all my joys and fears —even those about my father. Busy with his surgical practice, my father hadn't noticed that I had come down with rickets from an insufficiency of Vitamin D. Ala took me out into the sunshine to replenish my store of the vitamin. In retrospect, I think Mama was a bit jealous of my closeness to her. Ala married David Wilner two weeks before my fourth birthday in March 1939. Chana Liba and my Uncle Henry came to Warsaw for the wedding. Unbeknownst to us, this would be our last celebration as a unified family. My uncles in America tried to convince the family to immigrate to the States because they were concerned with the rise of anti-Semitism in Germany. My grand-father, Avram Zablocki, maintained, however, that if millions of Jews in Europe were not worried about Hitler, why should we be? So we stayed.

Life went on as usual, as it had for many years past. That summer, we even vacationed in a resort area in the country. It was only much later that we came to realize that we had been living in a state of denial. While we enjoyed our summer vacation, the world was rapidly changing, and our world was about to explode. After Poland fell in 1939, my grandfather made an astute observation. "Bad times are coming, my children. When Mirele, who has been such a poor eater, is suddenly hungry, I know famine is on its way."

He was proved right, as hunger followed the Nazi invasion and occupation of Warsaw. Proclamations were issued imposing many restrictions on the civilian population. The Jews were singled out with rules aimed specifically at them, including severe limitations on their interactions with Christians. This made our lives extremely difficult and dangerous. My family decided it was time to rejoin my father and uncles in Soviet-Occupied Lida and leave German-Occupied Warsaw.

So my mother and Ala packed our belongings in preparation for our journey. Mama tried to persuade my grandparents, especially Chana Liba, who was visiting us that summer, to come with us, but they were elderly, and felt that it would be easier to reunite at a later date when life quieted down. "Where are we going? Why are we leaving without my grandparents?" I asked. Mama explained to me that we would reunite in the future. I stood there crying at the thought of separating; they, too, were silently weeping. As they each took turns hugging and kissing us, I felt abandoned. Little did we know, as we headed for the border that divided the German-Occupied part of Poland from the Soviet-Occupied side on our way to Lida, that we would never see them again.

CHAPTER 2

The Lida Ghetto

When my mother, Aunt Ala, and I reunited with my father, and uncles Sevek and Tadek in Lida, we lived together in one house. I listened attentively as the men recounted their adventures escaping from Warsaw. They'd had no food to eat along the way, but Sevek had managed to find a piece of bread, which he willingly shared with Papa and Tadek. After a while, our lives seemed relatively peaceful under the Soviet occupation, and even took on a sense of normalcy. This was because Papa and my uncles had found good jobs. This was not true, however, for many of the 10,000 other Jews in Lida who had lost their businesses under Communist oppression. The Soviets had closed many Jewish community institutions and destroyed the Jewish economic base.

When I came to Lida, I was wearing the stylish short dresses worn by young girls in Warsaw. And I didn't speak Yiddish. The local Jewish girls wore long, baggy peasant dresses. They giggled and in a taunting, sing-songy Yiddish made fun of the way I talked and looked. "Hey little girl, why are you wearing such short little dresses?" "Don't you speak any Yiddish?" At first they made it clear that I didn't belong, but as time went on, they accepted me, especially when I began to act and dress as they did. And soon, the children in Lida even taught me to speak the *Litvish* (Lithuanian) dialect of Yiddish.

In Lida, my parents allowed me to play on the streets with the other children. It was so much more fun than in Warsaw, where play was limited to the park, and only under strict family supervision. In my group of playmates there were some older children, some in their early teens. One older boy took a liking to me and told me of the differences between boys and girls, and about sex. He wanted to play "house" with me, which included lying in the same bed. We played there but nothing happened. I told my mother about it and she in turn told my father. When my father heard of this incident, he hit the boy till he was black and blue. I was severely reprimanded, too. This incident was the beginning of many lessons on proper male-female behavior and discipline.

Despite the chaos growing around us, we lived comfortably in Lida. I remember how delicious the crisp white apples tasted in the fall, when picked fresh from the orchard, and how juicy the berries were. I felt that I did not lack for anything, except that I missed my grandparents. Mama and Ala wrote letters to my grandparents in Warsaw. But this became an increasingly difficult task, since the Nazis censored all incoming and out-going mail. Correspondence eventually became limited to postcards, which were easier to censor. My mother's friend Stella, who remained in Warsaw, looked in on my grandparents and often mailed their postcards. In the absence of my grandparents, I grew even closer to Ala, who lived with us. I could talk to her in confidence. Ala always tried to protect me from both my real and imaginary fears. She continued to be my "other mother."

In the summer of 1941, when I was six, the Germans attacked the Soviet Union. We again heard the roaring of low-flying planes—this time circling over Lida. They flew right over us, dropping hundreds of bombs. It was Warsaw revisited. I remember that day distinctly. It was early morning and we had not yet gotten dressed. Papa had already left for the hospital that morning and my uncles also had gone to work. Lying in bed near Mama, hearing the planes roar over-head, I instantly recalled the bombing of Warsaw.

"Mama, why are we being attacked again?"

She explained to me that the Germans were at war again, this time against the Soviets. I asked her whether we could escape from them again, as we did by leaving Warsaw. She just looked at me sadly. "Don't worry, Mirele, we will be all right. You must follow all my orders. Do what I tell you." My mother and Ala tried to decide what to do. Bombs exploded all around us and flames engulfed many buildings. Mama took me in her arms and told me that we had to leave the house quickly. We packed a few of our things and began running toward the edge of town. I was terrified as we ran. I kept thinking of two scary thoughts: "What if I become separated from my mother?" and "Where will I go without her?" I was most afraid of being separated from my family and left abandoned in the midst of confusion and chaos.

I held onto Mama's hand even tighter as these thoughts raced through my mind. I felt more afraid than during the bombing of Warsaw, perhaps because I was now older. As we headed out of town, we paused for a short while at a house that was full of terrified people. Just like us, they had abandoned their homes, and had gathered together hoping that they would be safe. It looked as if Lida was being burned to the ground. As the bombs came closer to us, we left that house and ran even faster past the outskirts of town. Panting and out of breath, we did not look back for what seemed like hours. At last we stopped and sat along the edges of the road. The light of the setting sun made the color of the sky all the more red, intensified by the smoke from the city in flames. Fires burning across the horizon made us feel vulnerable and helpless. I asked Mama what would happen to us next. She just held me for reassurance; she had no answers. We knew from what happened in Warsaw that more bad times were coming, especially for the Jews. Concerned about my father, I asked, "Where is Papa? Is he safe?" Mama merely nodded.

As the fires died down, we made our way back to our house in Lida, which somehow had remained intact, and reunited with Papa and my uncles. I hugged them, delighted at being together again. The retreating Soviet army was ordering many able-bodied men to report for military duty. Sevek received the call-up notice. He was unsure of what to do. Since failure to report was punishable by death, he packed up his things, and with great sadness, and holding back tears, he left to report for duty. As he made his way out of the house I clung to him, as I had clung to my grandparents when we left Warsaw. Neither he nor we had any idea of what awaited him, where he was being sent, or for how long.

The Germans bombed Lida again soon afterward, this time with even greater fury. Their grip on the city tightened. No house was safe. We again ran to the outskirts of town and watched Lida burn. On Friday, June 27, 1941, German ground troops entered the city. On Saturday, *Shabbos*, Gestapo SS and SD storm troopers arrived on the scene. They were sent to kill the Jews of Lida. This time we could not escape, as we had from Warsaw. We had nowhere left to go to evade the German blitzkrieg.

After the Occupation, German soldiers were everywhere. As a child of six, I could not understand the concept of war. Why were bombs being randomly dropped from airplanes? Why were the invaders wearing black leather coats with swastikas on them? Why were people being killed for no apparent reason? So many questions with no answers. I remember standing on the street with my mother as a German officer approached us. He smiled and lifted me into his arms. Brushing my hair with his hands, he told my mother about his own little girl back home. With her green eyes and small pug nose, Mama did not look Jewish. And as the officer left, we were thankful that he did not realize we were Jews. In these early days, of the ghetto, I would ask my parents all sorts of questions. "Why are we here? Why are we being shot at? When can we go home?" I quickly learned, however, that there were no answers to any of my questions. Exhibiting the naivety of childhood, however, I continued to feel secure as long as I had Ala and my parents with me. I could not imagine being separated from them.

Shortly after the German occupation of Lida, Jews were ordered to sew yellow stars of David to the front and back of their clothing. I did not understand why Jews were so different from other people that they needed to be branded. Jewish professionals were ordered to come forward and identify themselves. This group included my father. On July 5, 1941, most of them were murdered. Papa was spared because he was a surgeon—and therefore "useful" to the Nazis. A week later, a *Judenrat*, a local Jewish governing body of fourteen members, was established by the Nazis. Kalman Lichtman, a high school teacher, was put in charge. The Judenrat's job was to enforce Nazi directives against Jews. The Nazis also established a Jewish police force to carry out German commands—by force when necessary. All the orders ended with the threat that failure to comply was punishable by death. Jewish men between ages fifteen and sixty were registered and sent on work assignments outside of town. The working conditions under which the men performed hard labor were intolerable. The men were beaten regularly and threatened with death at the slightest provocation.

Women between the ages of sixteen and forty were also recruited for hard labor. The hunger worsened. Jewish laborers received a bowl of hot soup made of rotten potatoes, while most other Jews received even less to eat. Jews were forbidden to eat fat or animal products (meat, butter, or eggs). My father was immediately assigned by the German doctors to continue his work at the municipal hospital, and to operate on Nazi soldiers who had been wounded in battle. Since Papa's surgical skills were so essential to the

Nazis, he continued to be protected from the fate of other Jewish physicians, many of whom had already been murdered. Papa did not enjoy saving the lives of murderers. But he was closely watched, especially when operating on German officers. In the evening, when he returned to the ghetto from the hospital, he would smile saying "this was the first time in my career as a doctor that I enjoyed doing amputations." Papa was also dedicated to saving many peasants' lives in the hospital, and they expressed their gratitude with gifts of food at a time of famine. So we were hungry, but we did not starve.

The Nazis established a ghetto in November-December 1941, herding thousands of Jews out of their homes and into a dilapidated part of Lida as if they were livestock. The Germans limited how much the Jews could take along with them. Most of their possessions were immediately confiscated. We plodded on, grouped as families, under the watchful eyes of the soldiers, into the ghetto's small, primitive houses. The soldiers enjoyed pushing Jews around and laughing at them. The small house we were assigned to had four rooms and very little furniture. Each room housed at least two families, and several people shared each bed. We found ourselves both crowded and isolated. The ghetto had little food. Luckily for us, someone had planted vegetables near the barn behind the house and we could dig up onions and potatoes. I felt safe because I had Mama and Ala to hold on to.

An engineer and his daughter, Tuska, who was my age, also lived in the house. She and I spent many hours together playing. Along with other ghetto children, we played an unusual game. We collected paper labels from bottles and cans, usually extracted from the garbage, and traded them, much like children in America traded baseball cards. I had extra labels because my father worked outside the ghetto and could find me some new ones. Mostly, we stayed off the streets lest some Germans should suddenly arrive to capture, molest, or even kill us. Instructed by our parents to obey strict rules of discipline, we stayed out of harm's way. We dreamed of a time when we would be free to go where we wanted, to play where we wanted.

My mother and I often sat in the back of the house near the adjoining small barn, feeling caged like animals in a decaying zoo. Watching stray animals roam in and out of the ghetto at will, my mother observed, "How lucky those animals are. They have the freedom to roam where they want, where there is food, where there is comfort. These animals have more rights than Jews." It was sadly true. Jews were forbidden to walk on sidewalks, they had to walk either on the roads or in the gutters, and they could not be out on the streets when they were not working. Jews were forbidden to speak or have contact with non-Jews. Failure to report for work on time, by as little as even five minutes, was punishable by death. Jews were also required to give up all their furs, jewelry, gold, and other valuable possessions. My parents hid their wedding bands and some gold coins by burying them in the barn behind the house. As time went on, more people died from infectious diseases, hunger, and random, anti-Jewish killings.

One evening, a car full of Germans came to our house. The men with the black leather coats came in to take Papa away. I ran up to Papa and embraced him as he left, crying, "Papa, Papa, where are you going?" My father obeyed their orders and left. Mama and Ala huddled together that night, not knowing whether Papa was coming back. Did the soldiers need a doctor for an emergency in the hospital? Did they discover Papa bringing food into the ghetto? Miraculously, Papa returned the following day. He indeed had been taken to the hospital to operate.

In February-March 1942, as I turned seven, a major ghetto tragedy occurred in the Lida ghetto. Some 700 Jews from Vilna, attempting to avoid the even greater brutality and slaughters in their own ghetto, had managed to escape to Lida. The Jews in Lida's Judenrat, working with sympathetic Polish municipal clerks, were able to secure false papers, enabling the escapees to stay and work in

Lida. Among those Vilna Jews was a renowned Jewish surgeon who had helped train my father in Vilna. We welcomed him and his family and they moved in with us. We shared our meager food rations with them. Along with the arrival of the Vilna Jews, came a Jewish thief named Yaacov Avidan. Shortly after his arrival, he burglarized the residence of a local priest. The kind priest, who was trusted by the Jewish community, risked his life once the ghetto was established, by storing valuables for many Jewish families. The burglar also hit the priest in the struggle that ensued. The thief managed to escape from the Lida ghetto and returned to Vilna.

Both the Germans and the local Christians were outraged. The Germans then ordered the robber to be caught, arrested, and executed. The next day, the leaders of the Judenrat were summoned by the Nazis and ordered to turn over the thief, who had already escaped from Lida. All that the Jewish leaders could do was to turn over six other Jewish criminals whom they claimed had master-minded the robbery. The deputy Nazi commissar questioned the thieves about the robbery; they denied any involvement. However, to save their own lives, the robbers accused the Judenrat of making false documents for the Vilna Jews, to enable them to work. Avraham Virobek, another thief from Vilna, then confessed even more information to the Nazis.

In order to save their own lives, the robbers betrayed the illegal Jews from Vilna. At dawn on March 1, 1942, all the Lida Jews were ordered out of their houses and forced to march to the ordered location and to line up and walk between two rows of soldiers through a temporary gate where Avraham Virobek pointed out the 700 Vilna Jews; they were immediately arrested and shot the next day. I shuddered to my bones, in disbelief at the brutality of our Nazi captors. These men with swastikas and black leather coats were beasts and murderers. I held onto my parents for dear life, but in reality they could not protect me. Because it was a bitter cold winter day, some 200 sick and elderly Jews (including children and ailing parents) had stayed behind in the ghetto. When their families returned after the selection at the square, they found their murdered loved ones in pools of oozing blood. Luckily, no one stayed behind in our house.

Life was so perilous and unpredictable that no tears were left to shed. The ghetto existence, like terminal cancer, was a type of slow death, and those who were in it lived each day in fear, anticipating their own imminent demise. Surely our turn to die would soon come. I was by now fairly disciplined in hiding my emotions. This did not mean that I didn't feel them; I had just become more adept at controlling them. Living so close to death made dying a part of living.

To further punish the Jews of Lida for protecting the Vilna Jews, all the members of the Judenrat were tortured beyond recognition and then killed. Their bodies were defaced to the point that the Jews assigned to bury them could no longer identify them. New decrees were imposed to test the obedience of the Jews in the ghetto. Jews had to give up all copper objects and electrical fittings, and electricity to the ghetto was shut down. Ever since the murders of the Vilna Jews, we had developed a real nagging fear and paranoia. Every day at dawn, we looked out the windows to check if the Germans were coming. If the coast was clear, we knew that this day was ours to live. At night, however, we wondered whether the soldiers would be back the next morning. We lived one day at a time. There was no security beyond that. Fear, disease, and malnutrition also pervaded our daily existence. To placate the Germans, the Jews proposed setting up workshops of light industry to produce objects useful to the Nazis. Lida had many gifted and experienced artisans and craftsmen, and the Germans agreed to the idea. Small work factories were organized in a nearby technical school to manufacture shoes, electrical supplies, clothing, paintings, toys, bags, and other items. A Jewish engineer named Altman and a merchant named Alperstein were the leaders behind the idea and in charge of setting up and running the projects.

In early May, rumors began circulating that a major German "*aktion*" was about to occur. Not even Altman the engineer could extract information from the Germans on the validity of these rumors. The ghetto was sealed on May 7, 1942 and surrounded by police and gendarmes. On May 8, 1942, the great Jewish massacre of Lida took place. It was the crack of dawn of a very cold day. The snow had not yet melted. The ghetto was surrounded by Gestapo SD and SS storm troopers, together with their local collaborators and sympathizers. They came like butchers lusting for blood, Jewish blood, screaming their orders for the Jews to get out into the street. They hit us with metal pipes and with the butts of their guns. Many of the Jews were not yet fully dressed; some were still barefoot. Children cried in their mothers' arms. Terror, panic, and fear consumed us. I remember Mama grabbing my coat and shoes and socks. Once in the street, Mama tried to help a woman cover her little baby. She was hit from behind and forced to retreat. I clung to my parents for dear life. We were then ordered to assemble as families and march to an unknown destination.

We exited the ghetto and walked past the adjacent Jewish cemetery and beyond the outskirts of Lida. The old and the sick who could not keep up were shot on the spot. The bleeding dead covered the road with trails of red. We walked in silence, knowing that something even more terrible awaited us at the end of the march. What we did not know was the extent of the anticipated Nazi killings. At midday, we were about 2 kilometers out of town, when the line stopped for a brief moment, we could hear machine guns firing in the distance. As we came to an intersection of two country roads, the *Gebietskommissar* (German district commissioner), together with the engineer Altman and the Waffen SS and SD storm troopers, examined our papers and waved us on in one of two directions. At first, essential professionals who worked in Altman's factories were spared. However, after certain quotas had been met, most of the rest of the Jews were indiscriminately selected to die. Ala and Tadek, in front of us, were sent to the left. Before we realized what had happened, my parents and I were sent in the opposite direction, to the right, and the right represented death. The soldiers hit us from behind with the butts of their guns and with metal pipes to force us to run faster. Blood was flowing from the faces of those who had been hit from the front. As we ran, the sound of gunfire was getting louder and closer. My parents held each of my hands as we ran. My heart was beating in total fright as I looked up for a moment at their ashen and grim faces. We ran on with resignation, awaiting our imminent death somewhere up ahead.

Amidst all the noise and chaos, we failed to hear the soldiers yelling to us. One of them repeatedly

shouted, "*Arzt zurueck!*" ("Doctor, go back!")
The soldier finally physically stopped us and
ordered us to return. My father wore an arm band
bearing a red cross. His surgical skills were still
apparently needed. For a moment, we thought that
only Papa was being called back, and that my
mother and I would be forcefully separated from
him, but they signaled that we were all to go
back. By the narrowest of margins, we survived
that day. In the meantime, we retraced our steps
toward the left and rejoined Ala and Tadek on the
other side. They embraced us as never before, and
we wailed in relief for being spared. Ala rubbed
my feet to warm them as best she could. How glad
I was to be with her again. We were soon ordered
to be silent, to lie down on the ground in order to
be counted. Next we were told to get up and bow
to the Germans in appreciation of being spared.

At dusk, we were led back to the ghetto. That
night the survivors desperately searched for their
lost families, to no avail. Light from paraffin
lamps helped identify those who had survived.
The *Kaddish* (prayer for the dead) was recited
with bitter tears. There was groaning. Life had lost
all meaning. The next day, groups of surviving
Jews were sent to the site of the massacre to refill
the slaughter-pits with earth. These trenches were
full of corpses and bodies that were still moving,
clinging to life, only to be buried alive. Jews were
massacred with the same ferocity as micro-

organisms responsible for an epidemic. We were spared only because my father was viewed as still useful. A man named Fishel Beloborod was wounded during the massacre and left for dead. When he regained consciousness he got out of the pit and came back to the ghetto to inform us of what had happened that day. Those Jews who were sent to the right, some eighty percent of the Lida Jews, were driven to an area containing three large pits. First they were instructed to undress and enter the pits; there they were shot with machine guns and automatic weapons. Children were torn from the arms of their parents, thrown into pits, and killed with hand grenades; other children were thrown up in the air and fired on. Those in pits who were wounded died of suffocation. Shortly after the Lida massacre, Jews from the surrounding towns (Woronowa, Zoludek, Radun, and other small towns and villages) were moved into the ghetto, as entire geographical areas of Belorussia were made *Judenrein* (free of Jews).

After the massacre, the workshops were enlarged and most of the survivors wound up working there. The Jews of Lida hoped to have their lives spared by making themselves useful and essential. My mother worked in a shop making leather belts and wallets. My uncle Tadek, a tinsmith by trade, worked as a welder in one of the workshops. As part of the Nazi propaganda campaign, the German press came all the way from Berlin to photograph and document the productivity of these Jewish factories in serving the Third Reich.

As both my parents and Ala and Tadek were away working, I felt particularly scared and vulnerable being left alone with the other children in the ghetto. What if the Germans came while my family was gone, to kill all the old people and children? Would I be safe there? What if my parents were killed outside the ghetto? What if they never came back to be with me? Life went on in this fashion, day after day, week after week. In the summer of 1942, a rumor began circulating that all Jewish children would be murdered while their parents were away at work. My parents, together with Ala and Tadek, grimly pondered our options. It was an unbearable event to contemplate. My mother was very direct.

"Mirele, the Germans may be coming to kill all the Jewish children in the ghetto," she told me. My body cramped in anticipation of the events that would follow. Now, even my parents were helpless to protect me. "Papa will be taking you to the hospital. When you get there, you must act sick." The next day, I was admitted to the infectious ward, and my father injected me with several shots that made me feel sick to my stomach.

"Lay still," he instructed me. "Sleep as much as

you can. And when you are awake, keep your eyes closed and pretend to be asleep." I did feel sick, and I did sleep most of the time, but I did not have a fever. Several days later, the nurses began to ask Papa what was really ailing me. Their suspicions made Papa realize that it was not safe for me to remain on the ward. Nor, of course, was it safe for me to be exposed to infectious diseases. In the meantime, Papa had contacted a Catholic peasant widow whose little daughter he had rescued from death. After explaining the situation to her, he convinced the woman to allow me to stay with her. She lived on a farm several kilometers from Lida. A few days later, Papa told me of the arrangement he had made.

What I had most dreaded was about to happen. I would be abandoned by my parents to die without them, all alone in an unknown place. Before I could react, my parents took me to the side entrance of the hospital grounds. There, beside a stand of trees, a man awaited me. My parents handed me a small satchel of my clothing. I stared at them in disbelief. Seemingly unperturbed but crying inside, my parents bombarded me with final instructions for my new way of life.

"Listen and be quiet. Do whatever you must to stay alive. Never speak Yiddish, from this day on you are no longer a Jew. Pretend that you are an orphan and the woman's niece. Play with her little girl and help do chores. Stay vigilant and careful not to reveal your real identity. God willing, we will reunite in the future."

The instructions went on and on, each word more painful than the one that preceded it. I shuddered in dread and fear. For me, separation was far worse than death. In the haste of the situation, I did not have the time to tell my parents how I felt, and I was too numb to speak. They each gave me a last hug, and then let go. The stranger took my hand and tugged me along with him. As he dragged me, I thought of pulling free and running back, but he held me too tightly for that. I was completely distraught, but I held back my tears. I told myself that I had to be brave and do as I was told. I had been taught to follow orders, and now I was obeying them. I wondered whether this was the last time I would ever see my parents. I walked in total silence that sunny afternoon. The man tried to strike up a dialogue with me, but I was confused and angry at being abandoned, and far too traumatized to speak.

By dusk, after several hours of walking, we came to the farmhouse. The woman told her little girl, who was a couple of years younger than I, that I was her niece, and that I would be staying with them for a while. She told her that I was her new playmate. "Mirka is seven," the woman said. "She will help care for you and play with you while I work at harvesting the summer crop."

I was given a bed on which I promptly went to

sleep after a trying and tiring day. The next morning I woke up with the roosters. As I opened my eyes, I realized that I was no longer with my parents, and I started to cry. I knew that I could not give myself away, so I washed my face and wiped away the tears. Trying to act cheerful, I began my new life. I was given a good breakfast from the abundant food on the farm. I tried to help the woman with her chores, and I also played with her little daughter. I was always on guard should any nearby farmers come by for a visit. My biggest worry was my dark Semitic features, which contrasted sharply with those of my blue-eyed and blond-haired new family.

I remember being stung on the head by a bee. I was angry with myself for letting the bee sneak up on me like that. I was obviously not vigilant enough. The man who brought me to the farm returned with a small package from Mama. There was a letter from her, as well as some ribbons for my hair. I could barely read at the time, so Mama wrote it in large letters. It began, *"Moja Najdrozsza Mireczka"* ("My Dearest Mireczka"). As I read the letter under candlelight, my mother's words penetrated my soul. I could not stop crying for most of the night as I lay in my bed clutching the ribbons and repeating Mama's words, which I had memorized by now. I repeated to myself, over and over, "Mama, let's all die together. Don't leave me here alone." My pillow was drenched with tears, yet I could not stop crying. I carried on like that for days. I looked so tired in the mornings that the farm woman asked me if I were sick.

Several neighboring farmers came by at times. I dreaded their visits, fearing that they suspected I was Jewish. I tried to hide when they came, but it was not always possible, especially when I was doing outside chores. Once, the woman tried to take me with her daughter to the local church. I copied everything they did. I crossed myself, I knelt, and I sat quietly pretending to be praying. I realized it was important that I be visible, otherwise the others might think that I was a Jew in hiding. I could not understand why it was safe to be a Christian and deadly to be a Jew. Since I didn't know the difference between a Christian and a Jew, I could not understand why Jews were the objects of such hate.

After several weeks, it became apparent that the rumored killing of ghetto children was only that, a rumor. My parents arranged for the man who took me to the farm to bring me back to Lida. I skipped with joy the entire trip back. Papa came to meet me at the hospital. Overwhelmed with emotion, I jumped into his arms and began to cry in big heaves. Soon, my nose was bleeding with excite-ment. "Papa, Papa, we are together again!" I cried. "Papa, don't send me away again." We walked back to the ghetto, trying to avoid being spotted by Germans. As soon as I saw my mother, I cried even more than at the hospital. My grasp was so tight that it was difficult to detach me from her. "Mirele, it's all right," she assured me. "Mirele, we are together again."

"You won't send me away again?" I begged. "Promise me that." Concerned by our emotional encounter, Mama asked if I had been mistreated at the farm. I told her that I had not been. It was just that I was so scared of being abandoned. After the reunion with Mama and Papa, I started to cry all over again as I clung to Ala; I always loved her so. That fall, Ala and Tadek decided to return to Warsaw. Ala felt that her parents needed her, and that it was her duty as a daughter to go back. My mother pleaded with them to stay put.

"You survived the great massacre with us, and we have been through so much together. How can you leave now? Our parents are most likely dead by now," Mama implored.

"Please don't go, I love you so much, don't abandon me," I pleaded.

Our appeals were to no avail; their minds were made up. They contacted a nearby peasant who promised to take them back to Warsaw in his horse-drawn carriage. "It will be slow going," said the man as he gave Ala and Tadek peasant clothes to wear. In return, Tadek gave the man some gold coins that he had buried. With a heavy heart, we said our final goodbyes. I loved Ala more than anyone, and I could not believe that she was really leaving us for an uncertain future at best. That was the last time I ever saw her. The man probably robbed them and betrayed them to the Germans somewhere along the way to Warsaw, although it is faintly possible that they had reached Warsaw—only to perish there.

CHAPTER 3
Leaving the Lida Ghetto

After the May slaughter, the remaining Jews realized they were doomed to die. Nonetheless, they stood by not knowing what they could do to defend themselves. They had no tradition of arming themselves and fighting, and they also were too afraid of reprisals to undertake thoughts of an uprising. However, this same reality was the impetus for the formation of a clandestine group of some 120 young Jews who were able to secure arms from outside the ghetto. The desire for revenge against the Germans was the impetus for the group's formation. The center of their activity took place in the attic at 15 Kholodna Street in the ghetto. Some arms and ammunition came from the former Polish barracks, while others were purchased directly at exorbitant prices. Many weapons and their spare parts were also stolen. The group managed to assemble a collection of rifles, grenades, and ammunition with which to fight. A man named Baruch Levin, originally from Zholudek, led the group and operated a manufacturing workshop in the ghetto attic. He used his mechanical skills to refurbish broken firearms, and to produce weapons such as axes and knives. He was one of the leaders of the ghetto resistance. The group was able to collect 33 rifles, ammu-nition, grenades and other weapons.

The Jews in the ghetto were against the idea of an armed uprising. Many were convinced that work in the factories would save their lives. The armed resistors in the ghetto had therefore decided to leave the Lida ghetto and join the partisans in the forests. Working in the leather factory, my mother heard rumors that Jews in the ghetto were trying to arm themselves with guns.

"Partisans are operating in the surrounding forests," she reported. "Many of the younger Jews in the ghetto are trying to secure arms."

We had heard that in order to join the partisans, a Jew was required to own a gun. It was not at all clear how a Jew could escape from the ghetto, how he could secure a weapon, and lastly, how he was to find the elusive forest partisans. Mama also learned of small Jewish units in the forests that did not require that Jews be armed. Rumors were also spreading through the ghetto that caches of arms were left buried by the retreating Soviet army. Because new rumors were constantly circulating in the ghetto, few people knew which ones to believe, and besides, it was very dangerous to be caught with weapons. Anyone caught was subject to grave and vicious consequences. The process of securing weapons therefore was done in great secrecy. Often, parents did not know what their children were scheming. After the May massacre, many young Jews decided that anything was better than surrendering like helpless sheep being led to slaughter.

On Nov 9, 1942, the partisans in the Lipiczany Forest decided to bring a doctor back to the forest. They targeted Dr. Chaim Miasnik because he was renowned for his surgical skills. They also came for Baruch Levin because of his mechanical skills and the cache of weapons he had accumulated. The commander sent two of his best men, Nathan Punt and Yitzchak Mainsky to penetrate the Lida ghetto and bring them back to the Lipiczany Forest. I knew on that dark and cold December day that something unusual was about to happen. My parents stayed up most of the night speaking in whispers. They continued to talk in hushed tones most of the next day too.

"Heniek (my father's Polish name), to remain here is to die," my mother asserted. "You know we are doomed here. It's only a matter of time before we will all be killed." Since the ghetto slaughter in the spring, we had been gripped by morbid hopelessness and despair. Everyone knew that we were all marked for death. It was simply a matter of when and where. Still, my father was still not fully convinced as he continued to whisper that night.

"Broneczka, how can we take a child of only seven into the bitter cold of winter, to an unknown place?" he asked. "At least in the ghetto there is this house for shelter, a little food for us to eat."

"This may be our only opportunity for survival. We must go," Mama replied.

As I spoke with my friend Tuska the next day, I kept wondering what my parents had been plotting. Living in constant fear for our lives made us all suspicious of every move, of every person. Later that day, Mama took me aside and told me, "Keep this a secret, Mirele."

"You know I will never tell," I promised. But I wondered what was going on that made Mama so careful.

"We will be leaving the ghetto tonight, Mirele," she told me. "Some men have come to rescue us." I wanted to know more. I wanted details, but Mama quickly added, "Don't ask any questions. We don't want to arouse any suspicions. Mirele, don't hurry. Remember, act normal."

That afternoon, as I talked to Tuska, I felt extremely sad that I would be leaving her. I knew I would probably never see her again. There were so few children left for me to be with. It was unlikely that there would be any children in the new place. I felt fear, mostly of the unknown. Where were we going? Would there be Germans in the new place? Would we be caught escaping? Ghetto life was familiar now. In a way, however, I was also excited at the idea of leaving this place of suffering and imminent death. Maybe life would be easier in the new place, wherever it was. At least, I thought, my parents would be with me. I would not allow them to send me away again. As the grim winter day came to a close, I looked around me at the few filthy decrepit houses that were crammed with hopeless, sick, and hungry Jews. After the great massacre, our ghetto was confined to only two streets, Postovska and Kholodna. The angel of death would surely return and finish the job of devouring the last of the Lida Jews; any day could be that last day.

"Tuska, my mother needs my help," I said to my friend. "I will talk to you tomorrow." I hated to lie to her, but I had been taught the importance of discipline. A child in the ghetto develops all the instincts essential for survival. As evening approached, I saw Mama placing a few of our meager possessions (clothes, blankets, shoes) into two satchels. She made me get all my things together. "Do it slowly, Mirele," she said. "We don't want to arouse suspicion."

Well after the others in our house were asleep, we silently walked out into the shadows of the street. One behind the other we walked to a nearby house and quietly went in. People there awaited us. One of the men came over and ripped the yellow Stars of David off our clothes. Now I knew for sure that we were really leaving the ghetto. The men were apprehensive about taking me, a child of nearly eight, along with them. "What if she cries out?" one of the men questioned.

My father reassured them that I was well disciplined. "She is trained to follow orders. She will be no problem," he said. In addition to us, members of the Fleisher and Ilutovitcz families were also to be rescued. Sometime close to midnight, we left the house and quietly headed to the barbed wire fence surrounding the ghetto. The men used clippers to make a small opening through which we could pass. They rewired the fence so as not to endanger the Jews who remained behind.

We continued along a small river toward the center of town. At one point, we could see in the distance the lit windows of apartments housing the Germans. We were petrified to be so close to the enemy. Papa inquired as to why we were headed into town but did not get an answer. Suddenly, shots rang out. In total silence, the men motioned us to wade into the Lideika River and lower our bodies from view. Our hearts fluttering, we feared that we had been discovered. When the shooting stopped, we were motioned to cross the river to the other side. The only sound now was the chattering of our own teeth. Our wet clothes made us shiver even more.

Along the way towards Lida, we suddenly stopped. The men began digging. We had no idea what they were looking for, or how long the operation would take. After a long time, the partisans dragged out large bundles from the snow-covered earth, bundles that contained machine guns long buried by the Soviet army. The lights of Lida faded in the background as we finally left the outskirts of the city. Approaching the surrounding farms, a new danger suddenly arose. Dogs began barking. We did not stop, however, but walked even faster to avoid being discovered. Mama's legs froze up whenever confronted with danger, so Papa quickly placed her arm over his shoulder and helped her continue. I was almost out of breath by the time we slowed down in a thicket of trees. Under the glow of a large winter moon, we could see each other's faces. Mama remarked on my rosy cheeks and how healthy I looked. We kept going for several more hours. Finally, close to dawn, we arrived at a farm. The partisans entered the house without precautions. One of the men explained to us that the owner was a good Communist who cooperated with the partisans. We took off our wet clothes and hung them to dry, and then collapsed for a few hours of sleep. When we awoke, we were fed a meal of freshly-baked bread and white farmer cheese, accompanied by hot Russian tea— delicacies that melted in our mouths. Well-fed and dressed in warm clothes, we resumed our journey.

After crossing the partially frozen Niemen River, we walked ever deeper into the thick surrounding forest. The forests were so dense that little sunshine managed to penetrate through the vast canopies of pines, spruces, and deciduous trees. Thick fog often surrounded the heavy undergrowth and further reduced visibility. The trees stretched endlessly across the horizon, interspersed with streams and creeks that came to life during spring thaws. The impenetrability of these wilderness areas made them ideal hiding places for partisans. The Germans were hesitant to send their soldiers into the forests because they were so hard to navigate. In addition to the Lipiczany Forest where we were headed, other Lida Jews escaped the ghetto to join the Bielski group in the nearby Naliboki Forest. Our forest was extremely overgrown and desolate with limited road access, made of loamy soil with vast stretches of slimy, ice-covered swamps, peat bogs, and marshlands. Accumulations of snow, shielded from the sun by trees, made each step difficult, and there were no paths to follow. I asked Papa, "How do the men know where to go?" He had no answer but to tell me to be quiet and follow the others. Despite the unknown, we felt a sense of security; there were no more barbed wires or ghettos to contend with. At nightfall, we reached our destination, a camp of Jewish partisans in the Lipiczany wilderness. Our group had successfully escaped the ghetto.

CHAPTER 4
The Partisans

A fire was burning in the forest camp when we arrived. The partisans were glad that our escape from the ghetto went well. We were fed a hot meal of meat and potatoes, which was indescribably delicious. We had not eaten this well since before our ghetto days. I was surprised that almost everyone there spoke Yiddish. This is because I did not know at first that I was, in fact, in an all-Jewish fighting unit. How unusual to find Jews not caged in ghettos! As I looked around to get my bearings, all I could see was the vast forest of birches and pines with underbrush so thick that one could barely pass through. And yet all these men and women managed to live in the very thick of the wilderness. I wondered how they found the partisans at all, after escaping from the ghettos.

That evening we were assigned a sleeping space in an underground shed called a *ziemlyanka*; its entrance was a small hole. The *ziemlyanka* was like a cellar, an area in the earth dug only deep enough to sit or to walk bent over. It was lined with logs to insulate the floor from the frozen earth below. Wooden boards raised above the ground served as beds. The top of the *ziemlyanka* was made nearly flush with the ground, hidden by logs and ground cover. During the winter, it was covered with snow and was indistinguishable from the surrounding forest. A small fire venting to the outside, like a fireplace, helped warm our new home. The *ziemlyanka* was small and had little room to spare. We all huddled together in our assigned sleeping spaces. The closeness of our bodies was a further source of warmth, and it made us feel more secure. We fell asleep that night with hope in our hearts, and with a new sense of freedom.

The partisans cooked outdoors, careful to mask the escaping smoke that, if sighted, could give away their location. For breakfast a woman mixed flour and water and fried the mixture into pancakes. What a treat for a hungry child! I was overcome by the wonderful taste of this delicious breakfast. To eat such a meal in the ghetto was surely a crime punishable by death. As my hunger subsided, I began to wonder where the food had come from. I noticed that most of the partisans were armed with rifles, and some with machine guns. Innocently, I walked over to one group and asked, "Are you afraid of living in the cold forest?" They laughed at this young girl asking such naive questions. "We are not afraid," one responded. "We have guns to protect us. We are no longer living in the ghettos." Their answers made me feel safe and excited to be free. The very idea of the partisans was new to me. Seeing armed Jews not branded with yellow stars amazed me and also made me proud to be a Jew. I soon realized that I was the only child in the group. I asked myself, where had all the Jewish children gone? Where they all killed in the ghettos? I felt deeply saddened, and I thought back to my friend Tuska and the dwindling number of Jewish children still alive.

I still wore my old lamb's-wool jacket from Warsaw, from before the war. Under normal circumstances, I would have long outgrown it. The famine in the ghetto, however, left little flesh on my scrawny body. It still fit, although my arms were too long for the sleeves. Another treasure we brought along was an old blanket of goose down, from Warsaw. Our greatest need was for decent shoes for trudging in the snow, as we were in constant danger of frostbite. Mama and I quickly became integrated into the life of the partisans. We were assigned specific chores required by the group to survive in the forest. We collected wood brush for fires and we melted snow for drinking and washing. Mama helped cook. Despite being bewildered by the details of our new lifestyle, I continued to feel safe. At night, I would cuddle up to Mama and fall asleep in her arms. Papa was rarely with us. He was constantly sent away on missions to treat wounded partisans in scattered parts of our forest. Mama and I never knew where he went or how long he would be gone.

The partisan groups were initially established by young Communists who could not escape with the retreating Soviet army as the Nazis charged eastward. The German military offensive had been so rapid that many Soviet armaments were buried and left behind. The original groups of partisans used these arms to defend themselves in the forest. The partisan movement was established and run by the Communist Central Committee and not by the Soviet army. The partisan leaders were instructed by orders from Moscow to form sabotage groups to fight the Nazis. In time, operations became organized into distinct military units, each with its own commander. The groups were kept small and scattered intentionally. Mobile fighters were less vulnerable to capture by Nazi raids. High-ranking Soviet commanders coordinated the military activities of entire forest areas. The Russian in charge of the Lipiczany Forest was Stiepan Pietrovich.

Under him were six brigades, each with 1,000–1,500 fighters. Each brigade was in turn broken up into smaller fighting units of several hundred, called *otriads*. The partisans routinely raided a variety of German targets: troop garrisons, bridges, factories, trains carrying men and supplies to the Russian front, munitions dumps, medical supplies, and food depots. During the night, the partisans also attacked local peasants to secure food. Farmers who collaborated with the enemy were targeted, their stocks of food and clothing carried back to the forests. The peasants, held at gunpoint, were stripped of their leather boots and sheepskin coats. Those farmers who helped the partisans, the dedicated Communists, were not attacked. They made it more difficult for the Nazis to carry out their vengeful plans against the Russian populace. Search-and-destroy missions on unpredictable targets were especially dangerous.

Initially, there were no Jews among the partisans, but as Jews became armed, they joined existing Russian partisan groups. The survival of the Jews in the forests depended on the willingness of the Soviet partisans to accept them in their units. Eventually, all-Jewish fighting units were also established. Among the Jewish *otriad* leaders in the Lipiczany Forest were Dr. Yeheskel Atlas, Alter Dworecki and Hirsch Kaplinski (the brother-in-law of Baruch Levin). The Soviet commanders in the greater forest areas assigned the most dangerous missions to the Jewish partisans. To the Russians, Jews were expendable, a cheap commodity. For many Jewish partisans, killing Germans was an act of vengeance against the murderers who destroyed their families. The all-Jewish fighting units were eventually disbanded and integrated into Soviet units.

Jews who escaped the ghettos but were not

armed, mostly families with older parents or children, were not admitted into partisan fighting units. To survive, they formed family camps in scattered parts of the forest to elude detection and capture. While these civilian groups were extremely vulnerable to German raids, they were in even greater danger of detection by roving groups of local Nazi sympathizers whose mission was to capture Jews for a bounty payment, or just for the sport of it. Because the family camps were not usually armed, they had no way to secure food and winter clothing. Some had enough money or valuables to buy items from local peasants. Many were unprepared for forest life in remote and unprotected family camps; they suffered from malnutrition and froze during the winters. Most family groups were eager to obtain weapons from the armed Jewish partisans, with which they could steal their own food. Mostly, they depended on the good nature of some of the Jewish partisans to supply them with limited amounts of food such as flour and potatoes. Some partisan fighters, especially those who came to the forest with their families, parked their children and parents in family camps that were intentionally located near the *otriads*. The proximity to a fighting unit assured them both protection and intelligence of imminent Nazi attacks.

At mid-December 1942, some three weeks after we arrived in the Lipiczany Forest, we learned that a large contingent of German troops had entered our wilderness in an effort to capture and kill partisans and Jews. The attack was in retaliation for earlier attacks by the partisans. Dozens of Jewish partisans were killed in the battles that ensued, including the three Jewish partisan leaders (Yeheskel Atlas, Alter Dworecki and Hirsch Kaplinski). Also killed were a large number of Jews in family camps.

Mama and I quickly realized that we were not really safe. Here, too, we would have to struggle to survive. At the time, Papa was away on a mission, and Mama and I were left to face the danger alone. Frightened at our precarious situation, I asked Mama why the partisans could not defend us. Weren't they, after all, armed? She had no answer. The armed partisans reassembled into small groups and scattered away from the campsite into the forest. Mama took our few belongings and attempted to follow the armed men. They ran so fast and in so many different directions that we could not keep up the chase. Some told us bluntly that they would not take a child. That meant me, as I was the only child around. "What if she cries out and gives away our whereabouts?" they objected. "We can't take the chance of taking a child along with us. Any such behavior could alert the enemy and doom everyone." I finally understood why there were no other children in the group.

Soon Mama and I found ourselves with a small, barely-armed group of stragglers. As we headed further into the depths of the forest, we became hopelessly lost. We were now without protection, food, or water; all there was to eat or drink was snow. At dusk, as the temperatures plummeted, we embraced each other tightly in an attempt to stay warm. We rubbed each other's feet to avert frostbite, expecting to eventually freeze to death. The only way to ensure that blood would continue to pump through our bodies was to keep moving. As we trudged through the dense underbrush, not knowing where we were headed, we felt totally abandoned and panic stricken, especially after many days of aimless wandering. We did not speak much; my conversations with Mama were limited to our current predicament. I tried my best to keep up her spirits in an effort to prevent her from panicking, which I knew she was prone to do. "*Mamele*, we have to keep on walking," I urged. "Soon we will find the partisans again. Please, don't stop now; walk just a little bit longer. If you freeze up from fear then we will both die."

I was brave, but without Mama I would die alone. She in turn was afraid that I would die of cold and hunger. Her thoughts were of me. "Mirele, are you all right?" she asked. "Let me rub your feet a little." I remember one specific night, lying with several people in a pit under the branches of a large spruce tree. The branches helped protect us from the wind and cold. Suddenly, we heard noises in the distance. As they came closer, we realized that the sounds were footsteps. Then we heard men speaking German. Trembling in total fright, we could feel our hearts pounding. Mama held me tightly, my head buried in her chest. Was this the end? Did we come this far only to be captured now? Fortunately, there was no moon that night and the soldiers brought no dogs to sniff us out. They passed only yards away from us. Had they come earlier during daylight, they would have noticed our footsteps in the snow. We stayed put all night, our bodies shivering in the numbing winter cold. The only sound we heard was the howling of wolves.

One evening, we ran into several armed Russian partisans. "Now we are safe again," I said to Mama. "I don't know what to believe anymore," she replied. We gathered in an old abandoned *ziemlyanka*. It was too dangerous to light a fire, so we lay down sideways like packed sardines, one against another, trying to preserve what little warmth our bodies could generate and we fell asleep. We had not slept this soundly for over a week. It was too dangerous to fall asleep in the open forest; those who did froze to death. The next morning, we separated into smaller groups and again scattered into the thickest parts of the forest.

On one such day, I ran to the front of the line,

while Mama walked further back. Unbeknownst to either of us, our group had split in two. When I glanced back, Mama was nowhere to be seen; she had obviously gone with a different group. I found myself alone with four armed men. When they saw a child tagging along, they picked up their pace in order to lose me. I ran as fast as my legs could go. Panting and out of breath, I begged of them, "Please slow down, let me go with you. I will do anything you ask of me. My Mama is in the other group. My father is Dr. Miasnik. He is the forest surgeon." They ignored me. I quickly realized I had better save my energy by not speaking. I had to run after them, or else I would find myself alone in the middle of the vast wilderness. Without protection, shelter, or food, I would surely die and my worst fears would be realized—I would freeze to death alone. When Mama saw that we had been separated, she became desperate to find me. As the day wore on, we each wondered what was in store for the other. Would we see each other again? Finally at dusk, we reunited in the old *ziemlyanka*. Breathless and in tears, I fell into Mama's arms. The joy of our reunion fed our empty stomachs, as there was no real food to eat. I slept in Mama's embrace, secure for the night.

One night, the group of partisans quietly sneaked off, and we found ourselves alone again, at the mercy of anyone roaming the forest. We feared remaining in the *ziemlyanka*, as that would make us an easy target for capture by the invading Germans. Wandering in the night, we searched for a way to survive and avert freezing to death. After several days, we came upon another group of armed Russian partisans. Under the glow of the cold winter moon, we begged them to take us along. "Dr. Miasnik and the high command would want you to help us," Mama pleaded. "What if you were wounded and needed to be operated on?" They were unmoved, and instead they threatened to kill us if we tagged along. Again, we were left to fend for ourselves.

The bare winter trees cast long dark shadows on the snow. I looked up at the twinkling stars, seeking help from above, wondering whether we would ever be rescued and secure again. My stomach churned from perpetual hunger. My feet were numb. Lacking decent winter shoes, we wrapped our feet in rags. I kept asking Mama, "Why don't the men want us?" All that she could answer was, "War makes men act like beasts. We have to hold on as long as we can, Mirele. God will spare us if we are meant to survive."

After about 2–3 weeks, we heard from a passing partisan that Papa was alive and well. Papa had warned the men with him that, should they find Mama and me, they were to bring us back. And so we celebrated another momentous reunion, one of so many I shall never forget. Papa was amazed we had survived alone in the vast and cold wilderness, and so were we. Papa took us to a Jewish family camp located nearby. We had our first hot meal in weeks. Potatoes never tasted this good. As we lay side by side near a small burning fire, I felt safe again. I thought of the horror of feeling abandoned, but I dispelled these fears as I happily fell asleep.

Ever-present lice roamed freely over our bodies, biting as they moved from one person to the next. Lice transmit many infectious diseases, especially typhus. Periodically, standing half-naked in the snow, we squashed lice one at a time between our fingernails. It was a temporary solution to a persistent problem. Food was always scarce, limited to potatoes, onions and, infrequently, flour for baking bread. Most of our food was irregularly supplied by my father or a few generous Jewish partisans. There was seldom enough to go around; some days we went with very little food. We lived one day at a time, never knowing the source of our next meal and uncertain as to when the enemy would strike again. In addition, we were in constant danger from roving forest hooligans who would certainly turn us over to the Nazis if they found us.

One uneasy night, we learned that a group of unarmed Jews had been discovered by the Germans; news that alerted us to take precautions. At the same time, a member of our family group came upon a Jewish boy of about fifteen roaming in the forest. His entire family had been killed and he was attempting to survive alone in the forest, desperate to find a group to help feed him and provide him with refuge. He was brought to our *ziemlyanka*. The wisps of the fire lit his face as he tried to warm his frostbitten limbs. Though there was little food to spare, he was fed a slice of bread and hot soup. My mother and I had just been brought into the group ourselves for a temporary stay and were in no position to bargain for the boy's safety.

"Please," he begged, "let me stay in your group, I will do anything you want of me." The group leader replied, "There is no room or food to spare."

The members of the group knew each other from the *Zhetl* ("*Dyatlovo*" in Russian) ghetto and were unwilling to share their meager food supply with a stranger. The boy began to cry, and on his knees, he begged for mercy. My parents tried to intervene on the boy's behalf. It was to no avail. The boy was allowed to dry his clothes by the fire; he was then given some bread and led away by one of the men. He was taken deep into the forest, and a fire was lit to keep him warm. Alone and abandoned, he cried and begged, "No, no, don't leave me here alone to die." We never saw that boy again. To this day, I think of him with great sorrow and with much pain, as I remember how close I myself had been to dying a similar death.

My father was again called away to another part of the forest to attend to some wounded partisans. We did not know where he was going or for how long he would be away. When was a goodbye a last goodbye? During this period, my mother fell sick with typhus. She became progressively weaker as her fever climbed. A woman in our *ziemlyanka* took care of Mama. She laid cold compresses on Mama's body to bring down her fever. She tried feeding Mama some potato soup, but Mama could barely swallow. As her condition continued to deteriorate, I realized that she would soon die. My Mama, my companion and only friend in life, was about to be taken from me. I cried as I knelt beside Mama's bed, praying to our elusive God not to abandon us. Who would want me? Who would care for me? Who would be there to love me as she did? Who would be crazy enough to care for a child of nearly eight during a war meant to annihilate all Jews?

And where was Papa? He was always somewhere else when we needed him most. I heard two women whispering. They envied Mama's warm blanket. The vultures were already planning their move. The only consideration stopping them from any devious intent or from throwing us out of the group was the fact that Papa was their main source of food. In another part of the forest, Papa was chatting with a group of partisans sitting around a smoldering fire, unaware of Mama's illness. An approaching Jewish partisan asked Papa, "Doctor, why are you here when your wife is dying of typhus?" Aghast, Papa left immediately, taking along several sacks of potatoes. He arrived to find Mama critically ill. I looked into Papa's damp eyes and knew that a deep tragedy was about to unfold.

Mama lay there on her bed of wooden logs, pale and drawn, covered by her goose-down blanket. She had been drifting in and out of consciousness for nearly a week and was now in a coma. A raging fever consumed all her strength and energy. Papa injected her with some meager medications that he had on him. Helpless, there was little he could do. So as not to alarm me, he left the *ziemlyanka* and wandered out alone. I saw him at a distance, crying over Mama's imminent death. He tried as best he could to make her comfortable. Mama's fever climbed higher, she was now on the verge of death. I again became terrified of being left alone. I knew that Papa would be called upon to attend sick and wounded partisans elsewhere, and I would be left on my own, at the mercy of strangers. I thought back to that poor boy who was evicted from the group. I knew that with Mama's death I would lose my only friend and protector. She was my caretaker, the only one who would never abandon me. I cried alone, as Papa cried alone. To have survived this long, only to lose Mama now, was a possibility that we both found unbearable.

The night dragged on in anticipation of Mama's death. With lumps in our throats, we tried to sleep. As dawn approached, we checked on her again. To our disbelief, she was awake. Her face, gray in color and thin from dehydration, was smiling at us. Her fever was down, and she spoke to us. "Mirele, my Mirele!" was all that she could say. We were exhilarated that Mama had pulled through. As the day went on, my father became increasingly concerned that the long raging fever had impaired Mama's mental state. "Broneczka, why don't you sing us a song?" Papa requested.

Looking into my eyes, she sang her very favorite Polish love song, "I Know a Little Street in Barcelona." Tears rolled down my face listening to Mama. When she had completed the whole song without a mistake, Papa knew all was well. "Broneczka," he whispered as he kissed her cheek. We were relieved that the long vigil was over. The other occupants of the *ziemlyanka* were also pleased because their food supply was reassured. In those days, a doctor was far more important than a general. A woman in the group continued to care for Mama, and she fried tasty pancakes to build up Mama's strength.

Less than a week later, the Germans raided the forest again. We were forced to leave our *ziemlyanka*. Mama could barely stand up, let alone walk. Papa and another man held her up and helped her move along, her arms over their shoulders. We trod in the snow, covering our footsteps by dragging some tree branches behind us. We camped under cover of tall trees, over-looking a clear area from where we could see for several kilometers. Unable to light a fire, we shivered in the cold. Papa and I would climb up the trees, both to get warm and to spot any incoming danger. We hid for the next few days, hungry from the lack of any food. We finally received word from a passing partisan scout that all was clear, and we returned to our *ziemlyanka*. Mama's cheeks were rosy from the cold winter air and she looked much better.

CHAPTER 5
The Forest Hospital

My father's medical responsibilities to the partisans were extremely difficult to carry out. The toughest aspect of his work was getting to wounded patients in scattered and remote areas of the forest without having a rapid means of transportation. The sick were often too ill to move and had to be tended to on the spot. He had no attendant staff to help him, nor a sterile operating room environment in which to operate. He had no medications to ease the pain or prevent infection. All that he could offer the injured men was some vodka. The wounds were disinfected with alcohol, which was also used to sterilize Papa's hands. Papa carried with him a small satchel of boiled surgical instruments and cloths, hoping they would suffice. After the surgery, Papa would leave to go to attend to another wounded partisan, never knowing the outcome of his efforts. The treated partisan, because he was too ill to be moved, had to fend for himself during his painful recovery. There was a limit to how much Papa could accomplish alone. Clearly, a better way had to be devised to care for the sick. In response, the Soviet high command that oversaw the partisans proposed the establishment of a central forest hospital to serve the entire Lipiczany wilderness.

Building a hospital in the middle of nowhere seemed a preposterous idea at first. It was difficult to even imagine such an endeavor. To start, where would it be established? A scouting group organized and led by Dr. Julius Rosenzweig was formed. Because Papa was the only surgeon and the designated chief of staff, he went along to find a likely spot. The group eventually chose a small island completely surrounded by vast swamps, because of its remoteness and difficult access. They reasoned that such a secluded site would be difficult to find and capture in the event of German raids. For additional security, it was mandated that the hospital's location be kept secret from anyone not directly involved in its operation.

The challenges in implementing such a facility were enormous. The most difficult challenge was gaining access to the island. Building a real bridge with the limited equipment and supplies on hand was not possible. It was finally decided to float logs over the swamp, to serve as a makeshift but unsteady bridge. The wounded would be carried on stretchers, or on someone's back, over the logs. Sometimes, however, the carriers slipped and fell into the swamp, and great effort was required to fish them all out.

• • •

Living quarters were built to house the patients and the staff. One *ziemlyanka* was set up as the operating and recovery room, and a separate facility was erected for partisans who were ill with infectious diseases. Provisions had to be made for hospital beds, surgical instruments, lights (for surgeries performed at night), sterilization equipment, anesthetics, and numerous other items essential for administering proper medical and surgical care. Partisan raiders executed several missions to secure the needed supplies, obtaining most of the instruments, medications, and some anesthetics from municipal hospitals in the surrounding towns. Manpower needs were numerous as well. A cadre of doctors and nurses had to be assembled to administer medical care. The best source of such trained professionals was the supply of Jewish doctors and nurses who had escaped the ghettos. Many of the doctors took along all the instruments and supplies at their disposal. In addition, the hospital had to procure its own food supplies in the usual way, by raiding hostile farmers who collaborated with the Germans. These needs necessitated the recruitment of a cadre of armed partisans living in the hospital.

Papa was instrumental in choosing both the Jews to staff the hospital, and those to carry out the raids to secure food. About forty Jews were recruited by Papa to run the hospital. Jewish women from family camps, who were not partisans, performed the daily household chores. This gesture was a gift of life for them; they otherwise might have had no protection trying to survive in the forest wilderness. When the hospital was preliminarily in place, Papa came to our family camp to bring Mama and me to the new facility. Papa reassured our group that arrangements would be made to continue supplying them with food. We approached the makeshift bridge that was the entrance point to the hospital.

Following Papa, I skipped across the wooden logs with ease. Mama, however, was unable to cross on her own. Papa had to go back and help her. Her legs cramped because she felt scared. We giggled at her clumsiness as she held on for dear life. Our new *ziemlyanka* was designed to sleep about thirty people, mostly the hospital staff. Its beds were of solid wooden boards, with little space left over for storage. We ate inside only during inclement weather. Because of its privileged status, the hospital was stocked with more varied food in larger amounts than were available to us earlier.

I felt safe again knowing that I was living in a specially designated area guarded by the partisan high command. Living on an island surrounded by swamps afforded extra protection from discovery and capture by the enemy. I had grown to like the wilderness. By now I was an experienced hand, well adapted to forest life. For my personal safety, especially to protect me from rape, Papa shaved off my hair, and I wore boys' clothing that Mama sewed for me. Dressed in this fashion, strangers could not tell I was a girl. I felt safer and more powerful pretending I was a boy. Jokingly, the hospital staff remarked to me, "Now you look like a real partisan, Mirele." In spite of all these precautions, a teenage boy who stayed at the hospital for some time was on to me immediately. Papa hit him vigorously after I informed him that the boy had made advances towards me, and shortly afterwards he left.

Two Jewish doctors and several Jewish nurses came to staff the hospital. My favorite doctor and closest friend was Joseph Rakower. Of the nurses, I was closest to two of them, Sima and Sonia. In the absence of other children, many on the staff became very fond of me. Most of them had lost their entire families in ghetto slaughters. I became the generic child, doted on by many as though I were their own. In time, we all learned each other's life histories before and during the war.

Dr. Rakower's story was the most remarkable. An intellectual who spoke many languages, he obtained his medical training in France but returned to Poland to practice medicine. He married a beautiful woman who bore him a brilliant young son. The boy was as dear to him as life itself. After the Nazi occupation, the family was moved to the town's ghetto. Word spread that a massacre was imminent. Desperate, Dr. Rakower sought out some Jews who had constructed a secure hiding place within the ghetto. After considerable pleading, its intended occupants agreed to take in the Rakower family.

When he returned to tell his wife and son the good news, he found them both on the verge of death from a poison his wife had administered. She could not face going through a massacre and watching her family butchered. In grief beyond description, Dr. Rakower gladly went to the slaughter; life no longer had any meaning for him. As he lay face down in the mud awaiting death, a German soldier ordered him to stand up. Because he was a doctor (as evident because he wore a red cross on the sleeve of his coat), he had been selected to be spared. Upon returning to the ghetto, he discovered with great despair that the people who had been hidden in their special secure hiding place had survived the massacre. Sometime later, he escaped and joined the partisans in the Lipiczany Forest. There were many such tragic stories of lone survivors.

The nurse Sima, the future wife of Dr. Rosenzweig, one of the hospital founders, told another heartbreaking story. Sima was born in Belorussia and spent a year before the war studying in Palestine. She returned in 1939 only because she wanted to see her gravely ill father; he had already died by the time she arrived. Left stranded by the start of the war, she trained as a nurse under the Soviet Occupation of Belorussia. Her two younger sisters were killed in a ghetto slaughter. Sima survived, but she no longer wanted to live after the death of all her family. A friend insisted that she go with him to the forests. Because she was a nurse, she was sent to our hospital. The other women in the hospital envied Sima because of her popularity with the patients, who loved her tenderness and caring. When Sima contracted typhus, the other women staff that cared for her in the hospital discovered some gold jewelry under her pillow. This was a serious offense because she was supposed to have surrendered her valuables to the partisans. They reported their find to the hospital commander. Sima was threatened with death and was taken at gunpoint to the supreme forest commander, who was visiting the hospital at the time. She was pardoned only because my father stepped in and pointed out her value as a nurse.

The hospital staff included a Russian military chief who directed all non-medical missions, operating under direct orders from the Soviet commanders of the greater Lipiczany Forest. Our very first Russian chief was an ignorant and stupid man. He cursed the Jews in his drunken state. It was difficult to protect the Jewish women from his ever-active sex drive, especially when he went on a drinking binge. As chief of the medical staff, my father protected many Jews at considerable risk to himself. He safeguarded the women on staff from advances by the commander, as well as visiting Russian dignitaries, and also by the patients. When one of the Jews became sick, Papa sent him to bed and reassigned that person's duties to another, allowing for the smooth flow of operations. Thus, the Russian commander could not criticize the Jewish staff for being lazy.

It once happened that most of the wounded partisans in the hospital were Jews. Among them was a beautiful Jewish woman who had developed gas gangrene, a deadly *anaerobic* (lives without air) infection that grows in dead or dying tissue. Papa worked on her around the clock cutting the uninfected tissue to let in oxygen, so that the infection would not get worse, in an effort to save her legs. Our Russian commander accused Papa of giving better medical care to the Jews than to the Russians. A screaming brawl followed. My father swelled with anger. Red-faced, he yelled, "How dare you accuse me? I will report you to the high command. We will see who is more important in this hospital. I treat all the wounded with the same quality of medical care, Jew or Russian." Because this contentious situation threatened Papa's ability to do his job, in time the commander was replaced.

Despite the many challenges, the hospital continued to grow, and more facilities were built to house the operating room and hospital beds. The operating table consisted of a wide board supported on logs and covered by a sheet. Other sheets were hung to separate recovering patients from those being operated on. The hospital beds, also covered boards, were lined up along the walls of the hospital building, a log cabin–like shed. Pieces of cotton fabric and instruments were sterilized in boiling water. For surgical procedures conducted at night, flames from burning slivers of dry wood were held up over the wound by attendants or nurses to provide light. As the wood burned, ashes often fell into the patients' gaping wounds.

My most extraordinary experiences were watching my father operate. I almost never missed an operation, often staying up late at night. I saw him operate on hundreds of injured partisans. The wounded were carried on makeshift stretchers across the swamp logs and brought to the hospital. Riddled with bullet wounds and frequently writhing in pain, they were examined by the doctors. Hands were washed in soap that had been made in the hospital. They were further sterilized by soaking in alcohol. The patients were given anesthesia, if available; if not, they were knocked unconscious. The wounded areas were sterilized with alcohol. The other doctors and nurses assisted my father as needed. I watched abdomens being cut open and intestines exposed. Papa cut out the damaged areas, then reconnected the clean-cut ends. In more difficult cases, chest cavities were cut open with a saw or a knife and necrotic pieces of lung removed—some still containing lodged bullets. I watched as feet and arms were amputated with saws. Miraculously, most of the partisans who had been operated on survived their surgeries. Those who did die usually succumbed to infections. There were few facilities for those suffering from infectious diseases such as typhus, tuberculosis, and gas gangrene.

On one occasion, my father's life was directly threatened. He did not tell Mama about it, so as not to cause her to panic. A major Russian partisan commander had been severely wounded in the lung. He was brought to the hospital to have the lodged bullet removed. Another high-level Russian accompanied him and told my father in no uncertain terms, "Doctor, you had better pull him through. If he dies, so will you and your family." Luckily for us, he survived.

An unwritten but accepted law governed the safety of women. A woman who lived with a permanent man (husband, lover, or boyfriend) was spared from overt advances or rape by other men. The unattached woman was fair game for every man and was thus extremely vulnerable.

This reality led to many pairings of women with single men, in order to keep the women safe. Many remained as couples even after the war, including Dr. Rakower and Sonia, and Dr. Rosenzweig and Sima. Women made pregnant by the Russian partisans made up a significant portion of the hospital's patient population. They came for speedy and safe abortions. Some returned several times. Although I was not allowed to view abortions, I always knew one had been performed; a unique smell was always present following this procedure.

When it was too dangerous to transport a wounded partisan to the hospital, my father had a special horse that he rode to outlying areas of the forest. He operated on the spot, whenever it was necessary, without help from other doctors or nurses. Traveling alone and therefore unsupervised, he often stopped to treat and operate on sick Jews in scattered family camps. These Jews had no access to medical care and might otherwise have died.

The most dangerous jobs involved raids on nearby farms to obtain food. The men who carried out these missions returned with animal carcasses, flour, potatoes, onions, bread, and dairy foods. Because the hospital was staffed by Jews, Papa convinced the raiders to conveniently "lose" some of the food along the way back. The "lost" food went to feed the civilian family groups of women, children, and elderly Jews. Without this sustenance, many would have starved. Such tasks were undertaken in great secrecy so as not to arouse the suspicions of the Russians in charge.

On one occasion, the partisans returned with several live animals, including cows, sheep, and chickens. Among the animals was a little black-and-white lamb that soon became a pet to everyone in the hospital, especially to me. The animals were slaughtered one by one as food was needed. Finally only the little lamb was left. Some did not want to kill it; others, however, pointed out that sentimentality had no place at a time of war and survival. After much haggling, the lamb was killed. When it was cooked, I refused to eat it.

The Russian commanders enjoyed visiting the hospital. They liked to get drunk and shoot their guns off, just for the fun of it. They were dangerous to be with during these power orgies. The men often became restless and looked for new outlets to channel their energies. They especially longed for cigarettes. With none to be had, they rolled any available dried leaves into scraps of paper and smoked these instead. On one occasion, several Russian commanders were visiting at the same time. They began drinking vodka. On seeing my mother walk by, one of them offered her a drink. She refused, but he persisted. "You must try just one drink," he insisted. "You have to humor us today."

Finally giving in, Mama drank the vodka. She soon became unstable on her feet and began to sing. When Papa came along and saw what had happened, he dragged her out of sight, screamed at her, and finally slapped her. "We are alive because we are disciplined, don't ever forget that," he shouted. "How can my wife act so shamefully in public?" The thrashing brought Mama to her senses, and she went to our *ziemlyanka* to sleep it off. I was angry at Papa for acting so harshly, though I fully understood the need for discipline in these precarious times.

There were also more peaceful times, when there was a lull in the fighting and when there was less activity at the hospital. On those quiet evenings, we lit campfires and sang *Yiddish* songs from childhood, Polish songs, and Russian patriotic songs, as well as operatic arias. My father, a former member of a Zionist youth group, sang the Hebrew songs of Palestine. Papa and I contentedly smiled as Mama sang "I Know a Little Street in Barcelona," a reminder from several months earlier, when she was recovering from typhus. Some had tears in their eyes as they remembered their beloved families who had been killed in ghetto slaughters. We knew that life could never go back to what it was before the war, even if we were lucky enough to survive.

I recall one *Yom Kippur* (this is the Jewish Day of Atonement—the holiest day of the year), even though I had no idea what that day represented. All I knew was that my parents did not eat or drink on that day. I heard my father sing the *Kol Nidre* (a prayer in Aramaic recited at the beginning of *Yom Kippur*), a haunting melody that symbolized to me the very mystery of being Jewish, although its meaning was not explained to me. I assumed that not eating on that day distinguished us from the Russians. My parents always spoke of their lives as children with their own parents. They cried for their lost families who were probably all dead by now. I cried, too, for my Aunt Ala.

An unusual girl in her late teens was among our group. Her name was Itke, and she was a devout Jew who did not eat meat for the entire war, except when a cow was slaughtered according to the rules of *kashrut* (kosher). She mostly cooked potatoes, beans, and dairy products in her own small metal pot. As is the custom of religious Jews, Itke would not work on the Sabbath. The Russians liked to bait her and assign to her special chores to do on Saturdays. I remember my mother and the other Jewish women secretly doing Itke's tasks to spare her from punishment for disobeying orders. All sorts of arrangements were made with the Jewish men in order to protect Itke from being raped by the Russians. That she survived innocent and pure is truly amazing. Many years later I attended her wedding to a rabbi in Brooklyn. In retrospect, I realized that many of Itke's actions were unnecessary. Jewish tradition holds that, given a choice between life and death, one should always choose life. Therefore, surviving is more important than starving to death when kosher food is unavailable.

The hospital had strict rules protecting its entry point on the other side of the swamp. For security reasons, most partisans did not know its location. Those who approached it needed to reveal the secret password to be allowed in. I often went with Mama when she was on guard. Once, when several partisan leaders approached the entry, Mama of course asked them for the secret password. With her rifle pointed at them, she refused them entrance when they did not reply. I ran to tell Papa about it. He followed me back and spoke to the men. At first they were angry, but when they realized that it was Dr. Miasnik's wife who had pointed her gun at them, they apologized and commended Mama for being such a good guard. We teased her afterwards about this incident, because Mama often tended to freeze up when she felt threatened. This time, however, she was brave, like a good partisan.

Dressed in military pants and sweater, with my head shaved, I tried to act the part of a boy by working as hard as the men. I carried large wooden logs for making fires or for building new structures. I helped the nurses sterilize materials for surgeries. I sometimes helped the posted guards on the other side of the swamp, gathered wood, camouflaged trails, and scouted out the surrounding areas for safety. I had a knack for finding my way in the forest. I never got lost because I remembered specific details, such as bark colors of specific trees, unusually spaced bushes, and formations of trees.

I celebrated my eighth birthday in the hospital. What made this event so special was the gift I received. "Mirele, you are now old enough to have a gun of your own," Papa told me. I was given a real pistol for my birthday. Beaming with pleasure and surprise, I thanked my parents. "*Mamele*, *Tatele*, thank you. This is the best gift I could ever receive." The pistol had been confiscated from a German officer captured by a partisan. The officer had meant to give it to his girlfriend as a present, because it was small and dainty. I proudly wore it at my side in a special holster. In my boyish military uniform, with the pistol on the side, I felt like a real partisan, even though at first I was not given bullets. I wore it all the time, and it made me feel safe. Being skilled with my hands from early childhood, I often cleaned the machine guns and rifles that the partisans carried. I would take them apart screw by screw, clean them, and then reassemble them.

My mechanical skills prepared me for my eventual career as a scientist.

Dr. Rakower teased me daily about my pistol. "Mireczka, be careful not to shoot me with it!" he said. "Do I have to be scared of you now?" Dr. Rakower and I often played casino (a card game) together. At one such game, he bet me, my gun against his. I lost! He pretended to take away my gun and laughed as he did so. I did not find that funny at all.

Another time, while I went off to the "bathroom" (any appropriate hole behind some designated tree), I took off my pistol and hung it on the nearest branch. When I was through, I forgot to put the gun back on and left it hanging. Our Russian chief found it when he also went to relieve himself, and he decided not to tell me that he found it. I was terribly upset about losing my gun. "Mama, please help me find it," I begged. "Papa, you have power around here, can't you find it? After all, the pistol must still be in this hospital!" I was terribly upset by its loss for several days. Finally, the chief handed it back to me. He kept himself from laughing out loud as he issued a stern warning: "It is a crime for a partisan to lose a gun."

This incident was fodder for Dr. Rakower to continue his teasing. He even wrote a poem titled "Mireczka" to document all my numerous embarrassments as a young partisan. Dr. Rakower had become one of my closest friends even though his teasing continued long after the war.

Even in the partisans, acts of anti-Semitism occurred on a daily basis, with Jews being singled out by the Russian partisans as objects of suspicion and hatred. My father often got in the middle of such issues. In one of the large Russian brigades in our forest, a large number of Jewish women were accused by the Russian high command of being derelict in carrying out orders, and also of stealing. They were threatened with expulsion from the brigade. Expulsion had dire consequences, as it meant giving up their guns and, therefore, any ability to defend themselves. The women turned to my father to help clear them of the wrongdoing of others. Papa met with the high command to plead their case. Exasperated, he threatened to quit the hospital if the Jewish women were punished. "If you banish them," he warned, "you will be banishing me too." Papa was putting his life on the line and stood a good chance of being shot for this insubordination. The commander finally relented and the women were reinstated. Mama and I were proud of Papa for acting like a *mensch* (a man of honor) by protecting helpless Jews.

I remember a particular Jewish partisan returning to the hospital after a completed food-gathering mission. He recounted the story of a German officer who had been captured and brought back to the forest. Awaiting his execution, he requested not to be killed by a Jew. The executioner tied his hands and feet, identified himself as a Jew, and proceeded to chop off the officer's head with an ax. Another similar event involved the capture and disposition of a German officer by a Jewish partisan who had lost his entire family in Nazi ghetto massacres. Bitter with rage, he tied the German to a tree, gagged him, and cut off large pieces of his flesh with a sharp knife. As he did so, he declared in *Yiddish*, "This slice is for my mother, this one for my father, this one for my wife, these two for my children," and so on. Within every Jew was a desire to reap vengeance for the heinous acts the Germans had committed against his family.

On one occasion, after a fierce battle, many wounded partisans were suddenly brought to the hospital. My father was the only doctor around since the rest of the staff was away on other missions. He appointed Sima, the nurse, to be his assistant and instructed her to do exactly as told, explaining the details as he went along. Sima had never assisted in surgery. She was surprised and impressed that the operations went well and without a hitch.

Several days later, before the wounded had recovered, Germans in large numbers attacked the forest again. The partisan high command decided that the hospital was a potential target and therefore unsafe. As a result, the patients had to be evacuated and dispersed to separate dry islands scattered throughout the swamps for over a week. The hospital staff transported the wounded over areas that had no log bridges. Mired in the swamps and covered with leeches, the staff carried the wounded across on their backs. The sick were each given their "iron meal" (hardly the type one would feed to someone right after major surgery unless one had an iron stomach), which consisted of Papa's homemade sausages (he had learned how to make them from his father who was a butcher). Miraculously, all the wounded survived the ordeal and returned to the hospital.

Summers in the forest were mixed blessings. Summers were a time for picking wild berries and enjoying the sweet sap collected from birch trees, a forest delicacy. They were often worse than winters, however, because of the ravenous mosquitoes breeding in the swamps. Worst of all, summers were also the preferred time for the enemy to attack. The Germans would send massive numbers of troops to catch us. We called these attacks *oblawi*. The partisans had a well-planned reconnaissance system in place throughout the large forest areas. Partisan scouts were stationed inside rotten trees or in the branches of leafy deciduous trees. Others hid in camouflaged holes. Everyone was notified as soon as any Germans entered the forest. Often, when a

German soldier went behind a tree to relieve himself, he was quietly captured and brought back to a nearby partisan unit, where he was questioned at gunpoint about enemy plans in the forest. The Germans knew of these partisan tactics and were fearful for their lives after entering the forest. They also knew of our hospital and tried to find it on many occasions. During a German attack, it was dangerous to remain in the hospital, because we could not leave the wounded behind; unable to escape, we were vulnerable to discovery. In the last such invasion, the Germans attacked in especially large numbers. My father was forced to stay behind to try to evacuate the wounded.

During one raid, my mother and I hid nearby in a Jewish family camp. The group had built a shelter under a fallen rotting tree. It was massively camouflaged and undetectable from the surrounding groundcover. The entrance was a very small opening, into which a planted tree was inserted. As about twenty of us sat hidden inside, we heard approaching footsteps. Men speaking German walked right over us. We sat quietly, our heartbeats resonating in our ears. Silent prayers went up to God to save us again from yet another slaughter. The Germans never knew how close they were to Jews in hiding. I in particular felt lucky to have survived again. It was well known that in similar circumstances children were often smothered inside hiding places to prevent them from accidentally crying out and alerting the enemy. We sat in that shelter well into the night before daring to go out. It was one more very close brush with death.

Another time, as we hid among swamp marshes, a partisan came running to inform us that the Germans were coming our way. We hid behind the trees, our own guns pointed at our foreheads. We were not going to be captured alive. Better to shoot ourselves with dignity, and die by our own hands. At last, after a lengthy foray, the Germans gave up on finding us and left. Again we all returned to the hospital.

CHAPTER 6

Liberation

War proved to be a time when our worst nightmares were often realized. We would hear news of the life-and-death struggle between the Soviet and German armies on the eastern front. Partisan radio receivers described the slow German retreat from Moscow, Stalingrad, and Leningrad. I had no idea where these places were located; they were mere names to me, remote and far away. I could not envision the concept of being free and unafraid. War was not a time for pleasant dreams about the past or the future.

Preoccupied with staying alive, I no longer thought back to my life as a child before the war. This war had consumed five long years of my young life, and for most of it, I had lived in fear of being abandoned by losing my parents. Aunt Ala was a mother to me, and yet she left and abandoned me. I still missed her. Each day I gave thanks for having enough food to eat, for not being sick, for not being surrounded and attacked, and most importantly, for not being separated from my parents. Having lived for so long among trees, I was much more at home in the forest than I would have been living in houses on city streets. My life as a "boy" partisan, with my head shaved and a pistol on my side, now felt more natural than wearing dresses. My life, like that of other Jews, had been such a persistent struggle to survive, that I found it hard to believe we would still be alive to celebrate liberation.

In early 1944, just after I turned nine, and the cold winter gave way to spring, we heard the rumble of planes overhead. At first I was afraid of them, thinking that the Germans were coming to bomb us again. To our great surprise and delight, however, Russian soldiers parachuted into the forest. They carried notes with instructions that read: "In case of injury, contact Dr. Miasnik in the hospital of the Lipiczany Forest." One of the Russians was, in fact, injured and brought to our hospital for surgery. He told us that the Soviet army knew of the medical feats of Dr. Miasnik. They knew of my father's heroism as far away as Moscow. Mama and I were proud of Papa's stellar reputation.

Then in early summer of 1944, Soviet tanks entered the forest. As they advanced, they left behind them groups of defeated Germans, who now sought shelter in our forest. The swamps and forests that had previously protected us, had now become havens for the enemy, and therefore extremely dangerous for us. Fortunately, just as the Nazis started infiltrating our hiding places, we were liberated. News traveled fast within our forest wilderness: the Soviet army had finally come! Partisans from near and far converged to meet our liberators. We greeted the Russian soldiers ecstatically. Tears in our eyes, we hugged and kissed them as our saviors. Together with my father and the others, I saluted the soldiers. I kissed one in gratitude. As he embraced me, he complimented my father on his brave "son." Unfortunately, the Soviets forcibly recruited many partisans to fight at the battle front, then near the city of Bialystok in northeast Poland. Many died there, after having earlier survived Nazi occupation in the forests.

I was relieved that those ghastly Nazis no longer threatened us. Yet, I was apprehensive about what "normal" life would be like, and what new obstacles awaited me. It was a time of ambivalence, when the bitterness of war gave way to the sweetness of liberation, and yet the bitterness continued to haunt us in memories and nightmares. Our time of joy was also a time of sorrow for all those who had perished. For a Jew to have survived the war was nothing short of a miracle. This world still had a place for us. God had spared us after all. We became drunk with the spirit of life.

Along with liberation, however, came the painful realization of the dire consequences of Nazi rule and the full extent of its viciousness. With freedom came the news of the bloody extermination of Jews in unheard-of places and camps. In our part of Belorussia, the Jews in the ghettos were shot to fall into mass graves outside of cities and towns. In addition to the Lida ghetto, there was Ponar on the outskirts of Vilna, where some 60,000 Jews were killed; in Babi Yar in the Ukraine similar numbers were butchered.

We also heard of the final liquidation and evacuation of the Lida ghetto that occurred in September 1943. Early in the morning, the ghetto was surrounded by the SS, along with local police and armed soldiers. They forced some 4,000 Jews to the railroad station and over the course of three days loaded them into boxcars. All those trying to hide were caught and killed. A few of the Jews jumped from the train, however, and ran toward the forest. A Jew named Stolowitzki smuggled an ax aboard the train. A young man inside that car climbed on the shoulders of the others, squeezed through a miniature port hole on top of the rail car and lowered himself down the side of the boxcar. He used the ax to break open the outside door, thus enabling 14 Jews to jump off the train. They ran to the Naliboki Forest and became Bielski partisans. It is from them that we heard of the final deportation of the Lida Jews. After our liberation we were told that their final destination had been the Majdanek extermination camp, a death factory in Poland that murdered some 350,000 Jews.

Recently, an examination of Nazi records revealed that the Lida Jews had instead been deported to Sobibor, where 250,000 were murdered.

As I heard of the brutality of the Nazis, I wondered what had happened to Ala and Tadek. In my heart, I still hoped they had miraculously survived. "Wouldn't it be wonderful to see Ala again?" I asked Mama. "Do you think she may have survived? Is it possible we will find her somewhere?" She looked at me and replied, "Warsaw has not yet been liberated, Mirele. I doubt they have survived. Even if they got to Warsaw, they are likely to have been killed."

"Mama, I will continue to believe Ala is still alive, somewhere out there," I declared. "Don't miracles ever happen?"

Mama was especially sad because Ala and Tadek likely would have survived along with us, had they not left Lida. My aged grandparents in Warsaw had surely perished, but how, and when, and where? Was Sevek, my uncle who had been drafted into the military by the Soviets, still alive, and what of all our other friends and relatives? Even though we had been liberated, most of Europe was still at war. Jews continued to be killed in massive numbers.

After liberation, the Soviets sent us to a nearby hamlet called Szczuczyn in Belorussia. As I walked around town exploring the streets, a Russian officer approached me and forcibly took away my pistol. "I am a partisan," I said. He just laughed at me. I ran back home crying. Mama embraced me and quietly subdued me by saying, "Mirele, your little pistol is needed to kill Germans at the front." With that explanation, I was fully pacified. As long as my pistol was used to kill Nazis, the Russians could have it.

Liberation meant many changes in my lifestyle. I no longer needed to have my head shaved. As my hair grew back, I felt more like a girl again. I also started wearing dresses. Still, there lingered within me the feeling that I was now more vulnerable because I was a girl. As a boy in the partisans, I had felt safer and more protected, from threats both imaginary and real. I liked being a boy. It empowered me. During the war I had seen so many women attacked and abused. As I considered the merits of belonging to a particular sex, I realized that I ultimately had no choice in the matter. I found it extremely difficult attempting to reclaim my lost childhood. After all I had experienced, I no longer felt like a child. There were no Jewish children my age to befriend. I was suspicious of the Christian children, who I suspected would have gladly betrayed a Jew only a few weeks earlier, before liberation.

I soon met a Jewish girl my age called Halinka. She had brown curly hair and did not look at all Jewish. She too was searching for a friend. After we met, she recounted to me her story of survival.

As the Jews of the Lida ghetto were boarding deportation trains, her parents gave her an address of someone they knew in town and instructed Halinka, who was maybe seven years old at the time, to sneak out of line, go to the water fountain and disappear. Because she looked Aryan, she was successful in separating from the other Jews and running away. She was cared for by a Catholic family and raised as a Christian. Meanwhile, her parents, hoping that Halinka might survive, jumped off the moving train with the other Jews who escaped, and eventually made contact with the Bielski partisans. After liberation, Halinka's parents found and reclaimed her. Halinka was being pulled from both sides but reunited with her parents. I met her shortly thereafter. Listening to Halinka, I recalled my own life with the Catholic woman on the farm outside Lida. I wondered what would have happened to me had I been forced to live there permanently. The thought of it was too unpleasant to dwell on, and I let go of it as soon as it entered my mind.

The local Soviet leadership appointed my father chief of staff of the municipal hospital, and they assigned to us a house where we should live. As normalcy returned, the town officials attempted to locate the more educated people to serve as teachers in order to reopen the schools. I was enrolled in the third grade, even though I had no previous schooling other than being able to read and write Polish. The school curriculum was easy for me to master because some of the other children were as undereducated as I was. To please the local Communists, I became a member of a Communist youth group, the *Komsomol*.

In those days right after liberation, we viewed the Russians as our saviors. I proudly wore a red scarf around my neck and sang the many patriotic Russian songs I had learned from the partisans. I fit right in with the spirit of the *Komsomol*, enjoying being good little Communists. We often attended the local cinema to view Russian war movies. They all had one common theme: the brutality of Nazis toward the Russians. Typically, a pregnant Russian woman was forced to undress and run naked for hours in the snow. This torture was designed to make her reveal the hiding places of the surrounding partisans. Day after day, she was tortured. When the baby was born, it was killed by a German officer in front of the mother. Immediately thereafter, the Soviet army attacked the town and all the evil Germans were killed. We relished these movies because the Germans always lost and were killed in the end.

The Communist leader in Szczuczyn called my father to his office to announce that by an edict from Moscow, he had been awarded the *Orden Lenina* (Order of Lenin), among the highest medals bestowed in the Soviet Union. Mama and I were proud of this recognition of Papa's work.

Papa did not choose to go to Moscow to collect it, however. We were not content to settle for life under Communism, and we were now eager to get away from the Soviets. At about the same time, Baruch Levin, the Jewish partisan who had escaped with us from the Lida ghetto, was decorated with the highest medal of bravery, *Geroy Sovietskovo Soyuza* (Hero of the Soviet Union). Levin had blown up eighteen German trains carrying soldiers and supplies to the eastern front, killing nearly 900.

On a Sunday in August, as we gathered leisurely in the town square, a unit of Russian soldiers passed through Szczuczyn, heading for the western front. As we sat on a bench enjoying the warm sun, one of the soldiers approached us. He looked gaunt and weary from his long travels. He immediately recognized that my father was Jewish, and he began speaking Yiddish to us. In no time, we were exchanging life stories, a common practice among survivors. He glanced down at me, placed his hand on my head, and while gently stroking my hair, he inquired, "Is this your child?" When Papa nodded yes, the soldier lifted me into his arms, and began to weep. "This is the first Jewish child I have seen for hundreds of kilometers," he cried. "Thank you for saving a Jewish child."

Feeling his body heave with deep emotion, I put my arms around him and gave him a big hug.

It was not surprising to me that he had found no Jewish children. Most of them had already been killed in ghetto slaughters. I had no Jewish playmates among the partisans. And now, after liberation, I had found only one Jewish friend in all of Szczuczyn.

One day I was told that a card had come for us at the post office. I picked it up. The postcard was addressed to Dr. Miasnik at the town hall of Lida. Someone had correctly forwarded the card to Szczuczyn. The card was from Sevek in Leninabad in central Asia. I was so excited that I could barely contain my emotions. I ran to my parents as fast as my legs could carry me. "Mama, Papa, Sevek is alive!" I exclaimed. "Look, I have a postcard from him." Sevek had indeed survived, and an intensive correspondence followed. I wrote him postcards, addressing them in my best Russian to "Dear Uncle Sasha." He wrote that he had been very sick with malaria and was married to a Jewish woman who had nursed him back to health.

As our lives quieted down, my mother decided to go back to Lida to reclaim the gold coins that she had buried in the ghetto. We took the train to Lida and quietly walked into the section that had been the ghetto not too long ago. After the deportation of the Lida Jews, the houses had reverted to their original owners. The barbed wire fences were gone; there were no more Jews to cage. I had an eerie feeling in my gut as we passed by the house we had occupied. I thought of my ghetto friend Tuska, and I wondered how and where she died. Was she also deported?

The owners had a dog that kept barking at us. I wondered whether he could scent our presence. It was too dangerous to proceed alone. The next day, Mama located several Jewish partisans and asked their help on our mission. Carrying their guns, the men walked back with us to the ghetto. They ordered the owners of the house to raise their arms in the air. As the farmer watched, my mother entered the back barn and dug up the coins under the first step leading into the barn. The man apparently had dug in the barn on previous occasions, searching for buried Jewish treasure, but he had not found what Mama had hidden. Gratified to see the man squirm, we walked away with our loot. We boarded a train to go back, only to be told it did not stop in Szczuczyn. Mama was not at all worried. She offered the conductor a half-full bottle of vodka. "You can have it, but only if you stop in Szczuczyn," she said. "Just tell me where you want the train to stop, anywhere at all," he replied. Vodka was the best postwar currency, and it remains one in Russia today.

My years of isolation in the forest had some deleterious side effects on my health. Because I had been out of touch with other children, I failed to develop immunity to many of the infectious childhood diseases. First Mama and I came down with whooping cough. We were extremely sick for nearly three months. As required with this disease, we were partially quarantined. Papa took care of us. He was not very good at it, and most of the time he was too busy in the hospital to be there for us. While Mama finally recovered, I contracted infectious mononucleosis and, shortly thereafter, I came down with bronchial pneumonia. Languishing in bed for months, I became weaker and sicker. My coughing had become so severe that at times the handkerchief I used to cover my mouth contained blood. The bed that supported my body held me in place like a magnet. At times I felt as if I were wearing a straightjacket. Most devastating was my isolation; I had no contact with other children. I felt abandoned by the outside world. Halinka could not visit me for fear that she would become infected. Also shattered were my plans to go to school and learn. I was already so far behind other students my age. My recovery was extremely slow and I developed a persistent cough that was triggered by any physical exertion for well over a year.

With time, we became disillusioned with life under Communism. The system was corrupt and allowed little personal freedom. Anti-Semitism was rampant. Strict travel restrictions were imposed. Specifically, new edicts from Moscow denied those people deemed essential (such as doctors) the freedom to travel. We desperately yearned to leave these lands where so much Jewish blood had been shed, and where memories of the past continued to haunt us as gut-wrenching nightmares. We yearned to be free. My parents had two brothers each in America, so we were eager to go there and reunite with family. From my perspective, I could not even imagine a place on this earth that had not been ravaged by war.

As in the past, people who Papa had saved or rescued provided us with the opportunities for escape. Papa had befriended a colonel in the Soviet air force whose life he had saved through an emergency operation. Grateful, the colonel told Papa that he owed him a favor and not to hesitate to ask for help. It so happened that the colonel's brigade was about to leave for central Poland, as the front moved west. My parents decided to go to Poland because they wanted to get as far away as possible from the Russians, and they also wanted to see if anyone had survived. When Papa came to ask for his favor, the colonel assured him that he was ready to transport us to Poland on his military train. We immediately began to plan for our next journey: our escape from Communism. That journey turned out to be much longer and more difficult than we had anticipated.

(Top row) My mother's family in Warsaw in the late 1920s: Avram, Sevek, Bronka, Ala, and Ita. *(Bottom row)* Mama as a teenager, at age 22, Ala at age 17.

My father in Lida as a teenager, medical student, and as a young doctor with his mother Chana Liba.

Age two, with my parents in Warsaw.

My fourth birthday in Warsaw in March 1939:
Mama, Papa, me, Ala, my grandmother Ita, Tadek,
Henry and my grandfather Avram.

With Ala in a park in
Warsaw, 1938.

With Papa and Chana Liba, in Warsaw during the summer of 1939.

My cousin Sara Rosenbojm in the Warsaw ghetto in 1941. She worked with Vladka Meed to smuggle guns into the ghetto, and died fighting in the Warsaw ghetto uprising.

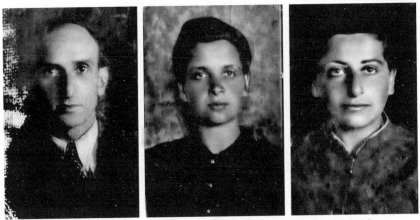

Papa, Mama and Ala in the Lida ghetto, 1942.

Age nine after liberation,
Szczuczyn, 1944.

My parents and me in Turda, Romania, 1945.

My parents and me in Rome, Italy, 1946.

Partisan doctors and nurses in Rome, Italy, 1945–46: *(Top row)* Drs. Chaim Miasnik, Oscar Rubenstein, and Julius Rosenzweig. *(Bottom row)* Dr. Joseph Rakower, and Sonia Rakower, Sima Rosenzweig.

My parents and me
when we came to
America, 1947.

My wedding to Henry,
Brooklyn 1955.

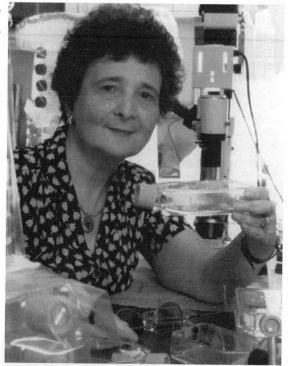

In my laboratory
at the University
of Texas, 1979.

Henry and me
after retiring to
Ann Arbor,
2007.

Havi Mandell and son David

Havi and Judy

Judy Brysk and Doug Elbinger

David Mandell

Sarah Mandell
Havi's Children

Hannah Graff

Benjamin Rocher
Judy's Children

Joshua Rocher

My family

138

CHAPTER 7

Escape from Communism

Mama informed me suddenly of our plans to leave Szczuczyn. I knew my parents were unhappy living there, but I did not expect us to be leaving this soon. "Mirele, we'll be leaving for Poland tomorrow," Mama said.

"But the Soviet army is also stationed in Poland," I replied. "Why are we going there if we want to escape from them?" Unable to get a logical answer, I finally said, "Do you think I am well enough to travel? I still cough all the time." Mama explained that we could not pass up this opportunity to leave safely. "Things are changing for the worse," she answered. "We may not be able to leave if we wait for too long."

We packed quickly and made ourselves ready to go. My parents carved out the lining of a wooden box and hid our gold coins inside. This money was designated as our emergency cash. I gathered and packed all my things in the morning, and in the afternoon, I went to see Halinka. I felt so guilty pretending that nothing new was happening, as if I just came over to visit her as usual. I had learned this survival skill when the war first started; keeping secrets was part of being disciplined. I wanted to hug her and say my goodbyes. I felt so sad to be leaving her without saying a word, just as with Tuska when I left the Lida ghetto. Each time I diligently followed orders. My ability to detach from those I loved and the indifference I portrayed made me feel like a traitor to my friends.

The next afternoon, the colonel sent a military truck to transport us to the train station. My father was seeing patients in a side room of our house when our ride arrived. He excused himself and then joined us as our belongings were quietly loaded. We lay down on the bed of the truck so as not to be seen leaving while our ride veered away from Szczuczyn. My parents were extremely nervous that Papa's patients would report our sudden departure to the local authorities, which did happen. The Russian secret police looked for us in the most obvious place, on departing trains. We were not discovered because they searched only the civilian trains, bypassing our military train. We later heard that Papa had been accused of robbing the municipal hospital, as a pretext for their search. Had the NKVD (the Soviet secret police organization later known as the KGB) found us, we would have been sent to die in some Siberian prison camp. We heaved a sigh of relief when the train finally pulled out of the station.

The Russian soldiers warmly welcomed us on board. They recounted their stories of battles fought and comrades lost. Together, we sang Russian patriotic songs and exchanged life stories. They were especially interested in our lives with the partisans. The trip was slow and uneventful. Two days later, we arrived in Bialystok, in northern Poland, and bid the airmen goodbye. We boarded a civilian train and headed south for the city of Lublin in central Poland. In Lublin, we made our way to the apartment of two Jewish brothers who Papa knew from the forests. They had lived at a family camp near the forest hospital. My father had helped feed them during periods of great famine. They welcomed us—at first.

A few days later, however, as the brothers and their families were preparing for a *seder* (the Passover *seder* is ritual feast that marks the beginning of Passover), it became obvious from their whisperings, that our presence was not really wanted. Papa was especially sad that the brothers had so quickly forgotten the many times he had rescued them from hunger. My parents were proud people who did not want to impose themselves on anyone, so they decided we needed to quickly find another place to live.

At this time, there was a shortage of available housing, and most of the newly arrived Jewish survivors were too poor to rent a place of their own. Because of this, many families would share whatever living space was available. One of these groups agreed to let our family move into an apartment they had just rented. We would be the apartment's first inhabitants. Once again, we gathered our belongings, and on the day before Passover, we moved in . . . proud and alone.

The new apartment was almost bare. It had several chairs, a kitchen range, and a toilet, but it had no beds or other furniture. Nevertheless, it was ours, and it gave us shelter. We had not celebrated Passover for over six years, not since 1939, before the war. As we huddled together, we remembered Passover *seders* with Ala and my grandparents. It suddenly hit us again that our families were gone, butchered somewhere in Poland.

"Mamele, I wish Ala was here with us," I lamented. I still cried and yearned for her. This *seder* night in Lublin was indeed different from all other nights, a night of painful memories of lost families. We lay down across several chairs and cried ourselves to sleep.

Famished in the morning, Papa went out to buy some food. As he went out into the street, several young boys threw rocks at him, yelling, "What are you doing here, Jew? Why haven't you been killed?" Papa heard them, and quickly entered the food store. When he came out, the hooligans continued their rock-throwing and anti-Semitic cursing. "We know what to do with Jews. Kill them!" they shouted. He managed to buy a loaf of bread and quickly returned to our studio.

He warned us to be careful. We decided that Mama, who did not look Jewish, would do all the shopping. Later, when I stepped into the court-yard to peruse our surroundings, I inadvertently walked out on the street.

"Another dirty Jew!" the youths shouted. I too was showered with rocks. I should have known better.

The Jewish families who had originally rented the apartment were slowly moving in. While there was little room to spare, we got along remarkably well with each other. Among them was a boy of about fifteen who was the sole survivor of his entire family. I looked up to him, and in no time we became close friends. He was not afraid to take me out on the street and ward off the Poles. He was tall and lean, with brown hair and light hazel eyes. When he looked at me and smiled, I felt awkward and bashful. His mere presence induced my heart to flutter in excitement. I had never felt like this before. When he told me how he felt about me, I confessed that I liked him a lot. Getting carried away by our deep feelings, we made plans to get together after the war. Naturally, I did not share my plans with my parents, afraid that Papa would hurt him if I did. In these still precarious times, the expression of intimate emotions seemed compressed into fleeting moments. At this moment, all of life's meaning was centered on my feelings for this boy.

For the first time I relished being a girl, not the "boy" with the shaved head. We shared many of our wartime experiences. I described to him my life as a partisan. "Would you believe me if I told you that my hair had been shaved to make me look like a boy?" He started to laugh with that wonderful smile of his. "I am glad too," he replied. It was hard to keep my feelings for this boy from my parents.

In Lublin, we finally learned of the events that led to the destruction of the various Polish ghettos. Three million Polish Jews had been killed. In March 1942, the Jews from Lublin were deported to the nearby Belzec extermination camp where some 600,000 were killed. Nearly 400,000 Jews were deported from the Warsaw ghetto to the Treblinka extermination camp. Those who were part of the Warsaw ghetto uprising were liquidated after the uprising in mid-May 1943. My cousin Sara Rosenbojm was able to navigate in and out of the ghetto, because she was blond and blue-eyed. As a Bundist youth leader in her late teens, she became a gun runner, working with Vladka Meed (a renowned member of the Jewish underground in the Warsaw ghetto, Vladka Meed survived the war and passed away in 2012) to bring arms into the ghetto. Sara died fighting in the ghetto uprising.

My mother decided to go to Warsaw to see what was left there. Papa pleaded with her not to go, but being stubborn, she went anyway. In her fantasy, she hoped that going to Warsaw would help her find her lost family. All of us shared the dream that someone in our family had survived and would miraculously reappear. Being so Aryan-looking, and speaking Polish with a Warsaw dialect, Mama was not afraid to travel alone. When she got there, nothing was left but ruins. Hardly a house was standing intact. The streets where we had lived (Zelazna, Sienna, Zielna) were unrecognizable, erased from this earth. Drawn to the site of the Warsaw ghetto, she wept for our murdered family: Ala, Tadek, Ita, Avram, and Chana Liba. All that remained of the ghetto were burned-out ruins harboring the ghosts of its vanished Jews. We later learned that my grandparents had been interned on Pawia Street in the ghetto and deported to Treblinka in 1942.

Jews had lived in Warsaw for some 600 years. A half million had been relocated to the ghetto at its inception. After the war, Poland continued to be a nation of rabid anti-Semitism and Jews continued to be hated there. On the train back to Lublin, Mama engaged in a conversation with several passengers on the train. They told her how much they hated the Jews and were glad that so many had been exterminated, but they were unhappy that a few had survived and were now returning to reclaim their properties. My parents decided that it was too dangerous to live in

Poland. Clearly, it was time to get out and settle in a less anti-Semitic environment.

Papa located a Russian soldier who was headed for Czechoslovakia. A bottle of vodka was enough to convince the soldier to take us along. That night we boarded a truck while the others in our apartment were asleep. Again I left without a goodbye, this time to the boy I so much cared for. I wondered whether there was any point in making friends, only to abandon them later. The Czechs were friendlier to the Jews than the Poles. We were now referred to as "refugees," and we needed identification papers for further travel. Clandestine Jewish relief groups were trying to rescue Holocaust survivors and made false papers for us for this purpose. There was apparently a problem with me because I was a child, although I was not told specifically what the problem was. I was instructed to travel without papers.

"Speak only Yiddish," I was instructed. "Say, when asked, that your parents are dead." We boarded a train for Hungary and waited until the police checked us out. When questioned, I answered in Yiddish, as instructed. Satisfied with our identification papers, the police left, and we resumed our voyage.

The Hungarian language has no Slavic or Latin roots and was totally incomprehensible to us. We could not communicate with anyone who did not speak Yiddish. Hungary too was viciously anti-Semitic. Berlin fell and the war finally ended on May 7, 1945, while we were in Budapest, Hungary. There were many street celebrations and parades to mark this epic event. People ran around ecstatic that Nazism and the Germans were finally defeated. For Jews, however, the elation was short-lived as so many of our people had already been killed by then. The ending of the war would not bring back Ala and my grandparents. It would not make the millions of dead Jews arise from their graves.

It was in Hungary that we first saw authentic photographs of the heaps of Jewish bodies in the various Nazi camps. We also met Jews there who still wore their striped blue and white concentration camp uniforms. They spoke to us of the mechanized processing of new arrivals to the camps. The Jews were transported by train, unaware of their fate. After a selection process to pick out those healthy enough to perform labor, women with children and the less fit were sent to specially-rigged "showers" and gassed with cyanide. Their bodies were burned to ashes in adjoining crematoria. The war had ended, but it was too late for most Jews.

While I had seen Jews shot in the Lida ghetto, those camp pictures were so incredible that I shuddered. My grandparents probably died in this way. I formed a mental image of my grandparents packed into cattle cars, transported to their death in Treblinka. This vision has haunted me most of my life. Sometimes in my dreams I can see Chana Liba, her arms outstretched, and I hear her calling to me, "Mirele, remember us." At a gathering in a large room together with the other Jewish refugees, a woman began singing the Yiddish song called *"Ich vill a heim"* ("I want a home"). Our eyes in tears, we listened as the song spoke of those innocent times when we were children, cradled in the arms of our parents. Ah, to be hugged and held by a *Yiddishe Mame* (Jewish mother).

I remember walking over to a scrawny old Jew sitting alone in the courtyard, still wearing his camp suit. I spoke to him in Yiddish. "Where were you during the war?" I asked. He was taken with my asking about the hell he had lived through. "What's your name, little girl?" he inquired. "Mirele," I replied. "Mirele, Mirele such a lovely name. Mirele, where are your parents?"

"They are here with me. We survived in the partisans." "Mirele, I was in Treblinka." His reply left me stunned. I told him my grandparents died there. "Mirele, have you ever heard the song 'Treblinka'?" he asked; "probably not." He sang it to me. It was the first and last time I heard it, but I remember it to this day. He sang of the horrors inflicted on the Jews in that infamous extermination camp. The song ended with the words, "Rivers of tears will flow, when one day will be found, the biggest graveyard of them all. Lying there are millions of Jews, *oyf Kiddush Hashem* (for the sanctification of God's name), in Treblinka, in Treblinka." I cried as I remembered Ala and my grandparents.

After several weeks in Hungary, the next part of our journey took us to Romania. Because of the uneasy political situation from the threat of Soviet occupation, we were taken to the border by train, and then smuggled over the border by foot. As the climbing became strenuous crossing the Carpathian Mountains, my coughing intensified. I could barely breathe. Many were forced to shed some of their meager possessions; they were too heavy to drag uphill. Once over the border, we boarded a train to Turda, a small mountainous city.

We moved with about fifty refugee families into a compound of several houses. We called our settlement of DPs (displaced persons) a kibbutz because of its collective lifestyle. We had a communal kitchen, laundry, eating areas, and other similar facilities. We were crowded in small rooms with little free space to move. My parents complained all the time about most everything. They later rented a small room in town, paying with money from our remaining gold coins. We moved out of the kibbutz because we desperately valued our privacy.

The local Jews from Turda were different from

what we had anticipated. They had somehow managed to escape the Nazi persecution, and they remained prosperous and were living in relative luxury. They were courteous to us and provided us with money and clothing. Impressed with Papa's credentials as a doctor, they often invited us for dinner. We communicated in Yiddish. I liked attending the local cinema, especially when I had learned enough Romanian to follow the dialogue. I also enjoyed eating the heavenly pastries from the bakery in the town square, nothing since has tasted as good. Paprika-spiced chicken and goulash were my favorite local foods. Romania had the tastiest apricots and oranges that I had ever eaten.

The kibbutz put together a musical show for the local Jews of Turda. I sang *"Rozhinkes mit Mandlen"* ("Raisins and Almonds"), an old Yiddish folk song my grandparents had sung to me. A local Jewish woman felt sorry for me and passed some money into my hand, in appreciation for my moving performance. I felt like a street beggar receiving a donation for singing my song.

My father had suffered from a hernia dating back to our time in the forest. When the pain became unbearable, he decided it was time for surgery. We went to the city of Cluj, where Papa was operated on by a well-known local surgeon. Mama and I lived in a rented room while he was recuperating. Just then, the Soviet army invaded

Romania. No matter how far we had traveled, we could not get away from the Communists.

Immediately after returning to Turda, we were ordered by the leaders of the kibbutz to leave Romania while we still could. With Papa barely able to travel, we boarded a train headed for the Hungarian border; our immediate destination was Budapest. Many peasants carrying small farm animals also got on the train. It was a hot summer day, and the foul smell from the animals became overpowering. To add to the misery, a group of armed Russian soldiers came aboard and evicted us from the train. They were eager to transport their own soldiers to Hungary. We next climbed to the roof of the train, but the Russians chased us off the top as well. Finally, to appease the rowdy farmers, they allocated two cars for civilians. A mad rush to get on board followed, with all the smelly animals adding to the chaos.

Because of the unbearable summer heat and the tight confines, many people began to faint and fall. Papa in particular, still weak from his hernia operation, decided he had enough. He got off and approached a car of Soviet officers. In his best Russian, he introduced himself. *"Tavarishch* (friend), I am Dr. Miasnik. I fought the Germans as a partisan in Belorussia." The officers were impressed with Papa's impeccable Russian and his service during the war. "Comrade Miasnik," one of them said, "we welcome you aboard." As

Papa boarded, he told the officers he had a wife and child. "Please, go and get them," an officer replied. "They will travel with us."

We joined Papa and spent the trip to Budapest in what felt to us to be luxurious comfort. Along the way, we were well-fed, and we spent our leisure time recounting war stories. I was warned not to say anything that might make the Russians suspicious of our escape plans, so I just listened. Our hosts were impressed with Papa's accomplishments. We began singing the Russian patriotic songs that we knew so well. We later learned that had we remained on the roof of the train, we would have been sucked off by the vacuum created when the train, moving at full speed, traversed the mountain tunnels.

We stayed in Budapest for less than a month, sleeping on the floors of a large palatial apartment house. There were far too many of us, however, in the allotted living space. We had little food to eat, and the most minimal of facilities. There were shortages of all staples because the Soviets had occupied Hungary and strictly regulated the supply of food. We explored the city and crossed the beautiful Danube. One side was almost totally demolished, while the other, where we stayed, was left relatively intact.

The Hungarian Jews were not at all hospitable to us. They made derogatory comments about the Polish Jews, treating us like third-rate citizens.

They did not share with us the food allotted for the group, grabbing it for themselves. Several spoke German well, and to them that somehow meant that they were superior to the Polish Jews, so they shunned us. As the petty arguments intensified, I could not comprehend how survivors of places like Auschwitz, the great Jewish equalizer where all Jews suffered the same fate, could still think that being a Hungarian Jew was superior to being a Polish Jew.

From Budapest we fled to Graz, Austria, carrying our usual false papers. My parents desperately needed money, and we were forced to sell the old down blanket that had kept us warm for so many years and through the worst times. The war had destroyed any of our notions of sentimentality; all that mattered was daily survival. With each illegal border crossing we left things behind. Only bare essentials were kept: a warm sweater, a change of underwear, and the like.

The Austrians hated to even look at us. Most were upset that we Jews had somehow survived. In this unfriendly atmosphere, we were happy that the Austrians had to suffer under Soviet occupation. "They deserve it," we told ourselves. Austria was the most clean and picture-perfect country on our long trek through central Europe. We enjoyed window-shopping there but had no money to buy anything.

We were then transported to a town near the part of Austria that was occupied by the Allies. During the afternoon, as our truck climbed the Alps, we came to a border-crossing in the middle of nowhere. The Russian soldiers had been paid off by the organizations helping Jews to get out from under the Soviets. One of the men donated a bottle of vodka, just to sweeten the deal, and we were able to pass. And so, after many months of wandering across central Europe, we were finally free of the Communists and safe under Allied occupation in Austria. Exhausted after having crossed so many borders under often adverse conditions, we had no idea where we were headed next or what our future would be. Each place was just another point of passage, heading into yet another new unknown. As "wandering Jews," we were no longer welcome in most of Europe, and we were a long way from anything we could call home. We had reason to celebrate, however, having survived both the Germans and the Soviets. We were free of them at last. While overjoyed at being "free," we had no home to go to, however. We were not welcome in Austria, any more than we were in the other countries through which we had traveled. The one positive point was that we were no longer surrounded by hostile Soviet authorities. Periodically, we gathered together with other refugees to sing the Yiddish songs of the Holocaust and to cry for our perished families.

CHAPTER 8

Refugees in Italy

It was the summer of 1945, and together with the other refugees, we found ourselves in a small town in Austria at the foothills of the mountains. The relief agencies ferried us from one displaced persons (DP) camp to another. These were not like the large DP centers that were established in Germany after the war. The ones we went to had no formal names; they were small, temporary makeshift operations. As impoverished strangers, lacking money and immigration status, and no longer citizens of any particular mother country, we could neither act nor travel independently. Our minimal needs were met, nothing more. All we owned fit into two small backpacks, and we lived day-to-day, tending to the necessities of daily life, never knowing what to expect next. With so many abrupt changes as rootless refugees, I had little time to bond to anyone, so I had no special friends. New people crossed our path, and most were total strangers. We shared one common bond: we were all wandering Jews who had miraculously survived a terrible war. We were totally dependent on the directives of the relief agencies in charge, and we had to trust that they were acting in our best interest. No one even knew where we were going next. The only certainty was the prevalence of rumors, and they indicated that we would be transported to Italy. I had never even heard of Italy, but I would soon learn the names of the different cities and countries as I traveled through them.

After a few days, a group of military trucks suddenly arrived at our compound. "Get packed quickly, and then get on board," we were told. Frightened by the sight of armed soldiers, we hesitated to obey their commands. We had good reason to be afraid of soldiers. We were flabber-gasted when they informed us they were soldiers of a Jewish brigade of the British army. Over-whelmed, we settled in one truck of a caravan of about five. Many of the soldiers spoke Yiddish to us, and their words were reassuring:

> "*Hot nit moiré.*" ("Don't be afraid.")
> "*Mir zainen Yidden.*" ("We are Jews.")
> "*Mir veln aich nemen mit unz.*" ("We will take you with us.")
> "We are here to transport you to safety in Italy. You will be well cared for, and protected by our soldiers stationed in Italy."

How could this be? The mere idea of Jewish soldiers seemed not just unreal but also preposterous. The last armed Jews I remembered were the partisans in the forests. To see Jews wearing uniforms and serving in a regular army was like a mirage to me, a vanishing oasis in the midst of war-torn Europe. Would a blink of an eye make the vision disappear? I was confused, yet happy that our rescue by Jewish soldiers was not an apparition, but a dream come true. We took off at dusk, headed for a free and unoccupied country. I stood in the back of the truck, mesmerized by the raw beauty around us, as we navigated the serpentine turns of the Alps. The moon was full and the view breathtaking. We arrived in a small military camp in northern Italy by morning.

Jewish soldiers acting against orders of the British high command brought us into Italy illegally as part of the *Bricha*, a clandestine operation that organized escapes and border crossings for Jews. Britain's policy was to prevent an exodus of Jews into Palestine. The reason for this policy is that Britain did not want to antagonize the Arabs, with whom it ruled Palestine as part of the British Mandate. These Jewish British soldiers were breaking army rules by ferrying Holocaust survivors into Italy for eventual resettlement to Palestine.

We were assembled into a roped-off area and sprayed with the pesticide DDT to delouse our bodies. We felt offended to be sprayed like a herd of animals. I supposed it was an effective and efficient procedure, but I didn't feel any cleaner for it. During the war we accepted the indignities we suffered because it was a matter of survival. Now that we were "free," the spraying seemed so out of place. To wash off the pesticide, we were handed bars of American soap that smelled like perfume, a real luxury in postwar Europe. Our clothes were also decontaminated. Many people did not own a change of underwear and had to cover themselves with sheets in the interim. For breakfast, we were fed army rations of Spam and packaged English cookies.

The sun shone brightly. The mountains, covered with deep lush green forests, looked so beautiful and innocent. They had not been eyewitnesses to killings and massacres. The air smelled sweet with morning dew. The sweetest scent of all was that of being free. Tended to by Jewish soldiers, we had time to take stock of our lives, and for the first time to dream about a future. It was hard to think ahead, however, without also remembering the past. The wounds of war ran deep, and we continued to be plagued by nightmares of death and the loss of our families.

While my parents sat down in the big army tent ready to be fed dinner, I wandered outside. At that moment, several Jeeps full of soldiers arrived. I noticed a tall and handsome corporal who looked familiar get out of one Jeep. He resembled my father, and I suddenly recognized him. It was

Josel, Papa's first cousin from Lida. I ran to him with arms wide open, calling, "Josel, Josel, it's me, it's Mirele!" He eyed me in total disbelief. As I jumped into his arms, he began to cry. "Mirele, is it really you?" he said. "Where are your mother and father? Are they alive?" As I was about to answer, my parents came out looking for me. They instantly recognized Josel, who was still holding me in his arms. He embraced them and exclaimed, "Chaim, Bronka, you are alive!"

Josel had been drafted into the Soviet army when the Germans invaded Lida. He was shipped to Russia in a similar fashion to Uncle Sevek. His wife and two children were left behind in Lida. After arriving in central Russia, he deserted from the army and made his way through Turkey to Palestine. Once in Palestine, for security reasons, he changed his last name to his wife's maiden name, Chwaletzki. He enlisted in the Israeli wing of the British army and fought during the liberation of Italy. After Italy had been liberated, Josel spent his time going from one DP camp to another, searching for any survivors from Lida, seeking any information about what befell his family. Papa was sad to tell Josel of the fate of his wife and children. They had perished in the Lida ghetto massacre. Devastated to have his worst fears confirmed, Josel was at the same time grateful that someone in his family had survived.

Josel drove us to an army compound in Mestre,

a town near Venice, where he was stationed. He told us to say that Papa was his brother, so that he would have more leverage to help us. Papa looked so much like Josel that it was easy to fake the relationship. The soldiers welcomed us and gave us a place to stay, spare military clothes to wear, and a set of toiletries. They did as much as they could to meet our immediate needs. As we sat among them, the soldiers described to us in Yiddish the features and attributes of *Eretz Israel* (the land of Israel). What it was like tilling the arid soil, and how the kibbutzniks transformed deserts into gardens. Above all, they told us how meaningful it was to live collectively as brothers on a kibbutz where everyone was Jewish. Jews were again embedded in the geography of antiquity, living in the very places where their forefathers had thrived in biblical days. At first, I could not grasp the concept of a Jewish homeland. I had no education, and I did not know any Jewish history. What were these "biblical times" the soldiers spoke of? I wondered whether they were making it all up. "Does such a place really exist?" I innocently asked.

"Mirele, it is our Jewish homeland. It is a place where children like you are welcomed with open arms," I was told. "What we most prize in Israel are the children. They are our future." How good it would be to leave the cursed continent of Europe and live in a Jewish homeland. The more

I thought about it, the more I yearned to go to Israel. I eagerly viewed pictures of Tel Aviv, a thriving modern city of light-colored apartment buildings. The notion of Jews growing crops on their own farms was new to me. In Eastern Europe, Jews were not allowed to own land.

The soldiers were interested in hearing how we had survived. My parents recounted our experiences under the Nazi occupation in Lida. But the soldiers were most taken by the description of our life as partisans. Josel was extremely eager to do everything possible for us, as we were his only surviving family. He took us to Venice and then by boat to the island of Lido di Venezia. The Adriatic Sea off the Lido was breathtaking to behold. Unable to contain our wonderment, we plopped down on the nearest stoop and stared at the horizon of pristine turquoise-colored water rolling in as gentle waves. The beach had few bathers because there were no tourists so soon after the war. Josel arranged for us to stay at a villa housing the Jewish officers. The officers treated my father as a Jewish hero and showered us with gifts. Ironically, since Josel was only a sergeant, he could not stay with us. One strange thing I do remember is that officers ate cantaloupe while ordinary soldiers ate watermelon.

We spent many lazy days wading in the sea. I had no bathing suit. Instead, I wore my best pair of panties. I watched children playing in the sand, making mud pies and building castles. They would never believe my war experiences. From time to time, I closed my eyes and wondered whether the beach would still be there once I opened them. I felt free and unencumbered, soaking in the splendor of my surroundings.

Several other refugee families also moved into the army compound in Mestre, so we were no longer the only civilians there. I often sat in the cafeteria eyeing the soldiers, in awe of the letters they wrote home. I had no one to write to. I was especially fascinated with their fountain pens. Almost effortlessly, the ink moved freely over the paper, and as it flowed, words and sentences filled the previously empty spaces. I wished that I knew how to write that well. Most of all, I wanted a fountain pen of my own. (My passion for fountain pens continued in America, where I began to collect them.) I asked one of the soldiers about his pen. Seeing my curiosity, he invited me to take lessons with him, including using his pen. "Do you mean it? You will let me write with your pen?" I asked. "I will not only do that, I will also teach you Hebrew," he answered. "In Israel we speak only Hebrew." My parents, particularly my father, were happy to see me take lessons. "Study hard, Mirele," he said. "You are lucky to have this opportunity."

The next day I strolled over to the helpful soldier's bunk, eager to begin my Hebrew lessons and jumping with joy at the idea of using his pen. He was a young man of about twenty with curly dark hair and deep brown eyes, and he looked so very Jewish. He received me warmly and offered me chocolate, one of my favorite snacks. I had not felt this good for a long time, and I hoped he would become my new friend. My last friend was the boy I left behind in Lublin. I wondered whether I would fall in love again, this time with the soldier. He was a good teacher, and I began to learn the Hebrew alphabet. Eagerly, I returned day after day looking forward to each lesson.

After a while, he suggested I sit on his lap, to make it easier for him to direct me on how to properly write Hebrew. While I liked the feeling of sitting close to him, I did not anticipate being fondled. At first I enjoyed it. It soon became obvious that he wanted to trade sex for lessons. I tried to ignore this realization, because I wanted him as a friend. Additionally, I was afraid of quitting because Papa would be displeased if I gave up on my Hebrew lessons. As the soldier pushed himself on me, I became afraid, and I stopped the lessons. I knew full well that I could not tell Papa about the soldier's advances. His knee-jerk response would have been to attack the man physically. Such a reaction by my father could endanger the warm welcome we had received as guests at the military compound.

When Papa heard I had quit, he turned red

and yelled while slapping me hard across my face. He perceived me as his "backward, stupid, and ignorant child." There was no way to gain Papa's approval. He refused to listen when he became this worked up. I was angry at him and at the same time terrified of his fury. When he left the room, I threw an object at his shaving mirror, shattering it to pieces. I wanted to shatter him into little pieces, too. These were, after all, good times for us, times to celebrate being free and well cared for. It appeared ironic and inconsistent that now, when our lives were no longer in danger, Papa would take out his own frustrations on me.

During the war, and later after liberation, Papa loved me and cared for me. Now, in quieter and safer times, however, his only concern became his own ego—his bewilderment at how a man of his reputation and stature could father such a stupid child. He kept repeating to Mama, "She does not know anything, and she does not want to know anything." For the first time, I began to experience incapacitating headaches. Mama was upset that I was feeling sick so often, and she would go out of her way to be nice to me. Even Papa took note of the headaches and became less critical of me. As painful as they were, however, the headaches served a good purpose. They made Papa less aggressive; as a doctor, he could understand real pain. I did not consciously know, until some forty years later, that I did not need to punish myself with migraine headaches. Once I understood this, they disappeared.

As soon as Papa began earning a little money taking care of the medical needs of the refugees, we moved into a rented room in a third-floor walk-up apartment in Venice proper. Our landlady's son was a medical student, and Papa tried to converse with him about medicine. As Papa's Italian was marginal, they communicated more in gestures than in words. In Italy, gestures are as much a part of the culture as is language, and as a result, they got along remarkably well.

The Italians we met had marvelous dispositions, delighting in the very basic elements of life: beautiful women, beautiful music, and hearty food. I sensed a romantic and dreamlike quality in them. Most remarkably, we experienced no anti-Semitism while living in Italy. Here was a country formerly ruled by a fascist government, one of the Axis powers ruled by Mussolini—yet the people were so gentle in nature. Where was the hate? Or had there never been any? It was many years later, while studying European history and art in college, that I began to grasp the cultural characteristics that defined different people, including the warring Germans and the peaceful Italians.

Together with Josel, we attended the opera and the summer outdoor concerts in the piazza. We were often roused late at night by a passerby's singing of operatic arias. Angry at first at being awakened, we soon became enchanted with music from *Tosca*, *La Boheme*, *Aida*, and *Pagliacci*. Josel visited often, bringing army food, clothing, and chocolates for me. I loved being with him. He was a generous and gentle man. He sensed my frustrations with Papa and he offered his comfort and support. I wished I were his child, the child he lost in the Lida ghetto; that way I would not have to deal with my stern father. He had a knack for being funny during tense and uncomfortable moments. I could always jump into his arms and feel safe. Josel was happy that I had become a Zionist in support of a Jewish homeland, and he loved telling me stories about Israel.

Dr. Joseph Rakower, now married to Sonia, the nurse from the forest hospital, arrived in Venice. I loved him even more now. He continued to tease me, reciting the poem that he had written about me. I did not mind it now, and I just laughed along with him. Dr. Rakower was a learned man, a real scholar, who spoke six languages fluently. He patiently sat with me to practice reading and writing Polish. Why could not Papa be this patient with me? I really did want to learn.

Soon good news came to the Rakowers. Sonia had become pregnant. They desperately wanted a child. They each had lost children during the war. Children provide a good reason for going on with life. Now they were both eager to move to a permanent home. At the time, pregnant Jewish women were allowed to immigrate to Palestine without being detained by the British authorities on Cyprus, and the Rakowers took advantage of this opportunity to move there. Before they left, they gave me a small leather photo album inscribed in Polish, "To the famed partisan Mirka Miasnik, in remembrance of the Lipiczany Forest and of Venice." As they left, Dr. Rakower shouted, "Mireczka, we will meet in Palestine someday."

Coincidentally, Josel was also leaving. His military unit was ordered back to Palestine. I was devastated, forced to separate from yet another person I had grown to love. My life experiences had led me to believe that separations were a form of dying, permanent breaks of precious bonds. As he held me in his arms, Josel whispered to me, "Mirele, we will soon meet in Tel Aviv. I will show you all of Israel. Shalom, Mirele, I love you." There was a deep void in my heart when both Josel Chwaletzki and Joseph Rakower left. I wished that Mama were pregnant, because then we could have gone to Israel too.

One Friday evening, we went to a synagogue in Venice, our first such visit since before the war. The building was old but simply magnificent inside. Surprisingly, it had survived intact through fascist occupation and Allied bombing. The chanting of the traditional prayers brought back multitudes of sad memories. A rich heritage of Jewish culture that had thrived in Europe for centuries had been all but extinguished in just five years. My parents began to sob, and so did I.

"Mirele, why are you crying?" Mama asked.

"I am crying for Ala," I replied. "I still miss her so much." All that I now possessed of Ala were memories and several photographs of her that survived the war. These miniature two-dimensional portrayals lacked her life and her spirit. Oh, how I had prayed that she would have survived.

Mama began writing letters to my uncles in America. I wondered at their reaction upon hearing that we had survived. I tried to imagine what they looked like and where they lived. My uncles insisted that we make every effort to come to America as soon as possible. They sent pictures of their wives and children and wrote to us often. Periodically, they also sent packages of canned food and clothing.

Mingling with the other Jewish refugees in Venice, I met Eva, a girl my age who was to become my best friend. Eva and I instantly bonded. She was pretty and slender, with blue eyes and light brown hair, which she wore in braids. Her most prominent feature was her ingratiating smile, and that is what drew my attention. Eva had come from Hungary with her parents, a grandmother, and a younger brother. Her family had survived the war in Hungary, but they escaped to Italy to avoid living under

Communism. In so doing, her father gave up a prestigious job as an engineer. Because of the extreme anti-Semitism there, Hungary was no place to bring up Jewish children. We both craved friendship, someone with whom to share our experiences and fantasies. Both ardent Zionists, we dreamed of living on a kibbutz in Palestine, happy to be taught Hebrew by Israeli soldiers while singing and dancing the songs of Israel.

We liked sitting at the edges of a canal, recounting our varied experiences during the war. "Eva, do you know that for my eighth birthday, I was given a real pistol?" I shared.

"Mirele, I wish I could have seen you with your hair shaved," she said. "You must have looked very funny. How did it feel to be a boy?"

We also revealed our deepest feelings, like how painful it had been for me to be forced to leave best friends without a hug or last goodbye. I described my friendship with Tuska in the Lida ghetto, and with Halinka in Szczuczyn. Eva listened especially avidly as I described my "boyfriend" in Lublin. I even dared share with her my impasse with the British soldier. The two of us laughed at even the most painful life events. We managed to find humor in tragedy. As we did not attend school, we had many free days to spend together. She had gone to school in Hungary and was relatively well educated for her age; I clearly was not. Comparing her accomplishments with mine made Papa angry at his own stupid daughter. Eva tried her best to shelter me from him. It was not easy for her to watch me being punished unfairly.

Venice was a magnificent city consisting of little islands surrounded by water. Eva and I spent days exploring the streets lining the canals. We liked to window-shop at the stores on the Rialto Bridge. We often visited the Piazza di San Marco with its bells, cathedrals, and museums. We explored the little alleyways barely wide enough for two people to pass through. And when someone paid for it, we loved riding in gondolas. There was so much rain that winter that the canals overflowed to the sidewalks; we giggled as we waded bare-foot in the water. I most enjoyed watching people living ordinary lives, perhaps because I wanted to live a normal life myself.

After ten months in Venice, the Jewish relief agencies sent us on to Rome, another move further disrupting the semblance of normal life. We were driven by truck past the city of Rome to a mountainous area in the suburb of Monte Mario. The hillsides of Rome were lush with pines, fruit trees, and large shrubs. Our new home was a villa on Camelluccia Street. After entering the estate, we drove through a long archway lined with stately shade trees. The house was a large two-story building located on about fifty acres of land. The opulent estate must have been owned by a wealthy Italian family. The owners were nowhere in sight, however, perhaps they had been killed during the war. Why else was it rented to refugees? My family was assigned two small rooms, one for my parents and a smaller closet-sized space for me. We were lucky to have this much privacy, because many of the larger rooms had to be shared among several families. Bathrooms were communal, as were the kitchen and laundry. New families kept arriving, some with children. Some we knew from the partisans or from Romania. We were reunited with Dr. Rosenzweig and Sima and their new son, Nachum; the partisan Joselewicz and his wife, Hadassah; and Dr. Rubinstein and his wife, Lucia. It was our own kibbutz—a forerunner to life on a real kibbutz in Israel.

An unusual Jew told us that he had a rich cousin who lived in Hollywood. He was angry at his American relative because he wrote neatly typed letters in English. "If my cousin Meyer really cared about me, he would write letters by hand in Yiddish," the man complained. "If he didn't know enough Yiddish, he could write me in English. But, sending me official typed letters is too impersonal. If my American cousin really cared for me, he would take time out to write me by hand." We were all curious about this American cousin in Hollywood. "Is he in movies?" Mama asked. "Oh, yes, Meyer is in business with two other partners," he replied. "His company is called Metro-Goldwyn-Meyer."

Eva and I continued to spend our days together. We explored the surrounding countryside by foot. We picked and ate figs and dates, grapes and persimmons, oranges and apples, each as they ripened. We played with her brother, Ivanko, and the other small children who looked up to us. Each of them had had interrupted childhoods and could not identify with the concept of "home." They were not used to being among other Jewish children. Many were justifiably suspicious of strangers. We communicated in Yiddish. Soon, Dr. Rosenzweig began to teach us Hebrew. He also taught us Hebrew songs and dances, in preparation for our eventual move to Palestine.

Unhappy at my lack of progress in getting an education at the kibbutz, my parents were eager to enroll me in a regular Italian school. To facilitate this transition, they arranged with an Italian young man, who lived in a small house near our villa, to teach me how to read and write Italian. I started going to my Italian lessons several times a week. While my Italian teacher was kind and far more patient than my father, once again, more serious problems quickly developed. My teacher became flirtatious, touching, fondling, and kissing me. Extremely uncomfortable with his advances, I attempted to convince my tutor that he was hired to teach me Italian, and that was all. Undeterred, he kept pursuing me physically. I wanted to end the lessons, but I was afraid of Papa's reaction. I eventually just refused to go, no matter what the punishment.

Mama, meanwhile, acquired two Polish schoolbooks to teach me biology and geography. My lessons with her went extremely well. She was patient and encouraging in her approach. I carefully examined the European maps to retrace the places we had lived and the journeys we had traveled. I learned the names of continents and countries, oceans and rivers. I also tried to learn the names of the states in America. They were such long and funny sounding names. I probably did not pronounce them correctly. My love for geography started my first real hobby: collecting stamps. I eagerly awaited the postman in an effort to find new stamps. I requested that my uncles in America send me letters with rare stamps on them. Eva and I shared our stamps, but we were shrewd when we traded stamps with the other children.

My lessons in mathematics and science with Papa were total disasters. He overlooked the fact that I knew little arithmetic and jumped directly into long division and algebra. He complained that I knew so little, and was frustrated that I did not learn what he taught me. He screamed at me ferociously and often smacked me in fits of rage. He even resorted to locking me in my room, especially on those days when the others were going to the beach, or for picnics, or to Rome. A lot of people at our kibbutz felt sorry for me, especially Eva. Eva resented Papa, and she never got used to his flares of rage.

Together, Eva and I planned ways of getting even with Papa. On one occasion when locked in my room, I managed to escape through an open window and clawed my way down the bushes from the second floor. I ran to the back garden and climbed to the top of a large shade tree. Eva brought me food to eat. From my perch I could see my parents below, running around frantically looking for me. Smiling to myself, I was glad to see them suffer. Maybe they finally realized the pain they were inflicting on me. I stayed in the tree for several hours, till early evening. When I finally returned, Mama was overjoyed to see me. "Mirele, where were you?" she asked. "I was terribly worried about you." I was hoping that because she was so worried about me, she would then begin to stand up for me and protect me from Papa; it was an unfulfilled hope.

It was not unusual to see more and more refugees attempting to have babies. Many Jews were desperately trying to make up for the children who had been killed during the war. I remember my father performing a *bris* (ritual Jewish circumcision) on a newborn boy. Certainly it was among the first on a child born after the

Holocaust. We celebrated the occasion with prayers and with songs. It was very special to witness Jewish children again being born, as almost no babies had survived.

Several Zionist organizations were attempting to recruit Jews to go to Palestine. In particular, they wanted my father to become director of surgery at the Hadassah Hospital in Jerusalem. Papa was tempted by this once-in-a-lifetime offer. After all, if he went to Palestine, he would not have to pass any qualifying exams to practice medicine. Mama, however, was adamantly opposed to the idea. "We are going to America because our family is there," she insisted. She was opposed to immigrating to a land where Jews were fighting for their independence. "After all we have gone through, we deserve a place of peace." I wanted to go to Palestine and become a part of a new Jewish nation. I yearned to live with other Jewish children who had also survived the war. I was a Zionist dreaming of living in a land promised to Jews by God himself.

I turned eleven in Monte Mario. As a birthday present, Eva gave me a special little fancy notebook inscribed with a poem she had written:

What shall I tell you
What shall I give you
I have such a short life myself
I have a heart that cares and feels

175

I love you Miriam
That is all I can say

Our friendship continued to grow, as we shared more experiences together—crying, and laughing ourselves silly. Because I was now older, the relationship was deeper than my previous wartime friendships. We soon started practicing a musical show to be performed by the children of the kibbutz. The younger children consulted us about their songs and dances. We often teased them; they took the ribbing rather well. The show was a big success and we did an encore performance.

Eva's parents became increasingly agitated with each other, endlessly arguing over the lack of direction for their future. After more than half a year in Rome, her father decided to return to Hungary. He had grown weary of sitting around doing nothing, waiting for something to happen and somewhere to go. He left alone. Eva and her mother decided to remain. It made no sense to leave one's family and return to life under Communism. Her father's departure was painful for Eva. She needed me now more than ever, as she experienced the frustrations of the breakup of her own family.

It was August 1946, in what had been a sizzling hot summer. The kibbutzniks were driven by truck to cool down at the beach at Ostia. Since it was hot and crowded on the beach, the trip did not achieve its intended purpose. Shortly there-after, Eva became sick. She shivered as her fever kept rising. My parents discouraged me from seeing her, afraid I would also become infected. Nonetheless, I sat by her side when our parents were not looking. Occasionally, I even cuddled up to her to warm her, trying to relieve her chills. "Please Eva, get better," I begged. "We will be going together to Israel soon. In Israel you'll be called Chava, and I will call you Chavele." She got progressively worse and was finally diagnosed with *bulbar polio*, a grave variety of the disease that paralyzes the breathing apparatus. On August 11, a week after she became sick, Eva died.

I could not stop crying as I hugged her mother and brother. I had never been to a funeral before. During the war, Jews were not entitled to funerals or to proper burials. I was grief-stricken seeing her coffin lowered into the grave. I was angry with God for Eva's death. I remember her with great love. After her death, the rest of Eva's family went back to Hungary. I am saddened that she did not have the chance to live out her life and fulfill her dreams. Every August 11, I remember her, to this day. This time it was Eva who left me. I discovered that being abandoned by a friend was as difficult as doing the abandoning.

That September, we celebrated *Rosh Hashanah* (Jewish New Year). It was our first holiday observance since before the war. Papa served as both cantor and rabbi at our outdoor service. With his deep and melodic tenor voice, he conducted the entire service. It was an unbelievably moving experience to witness the refugee Jews huddled together praying to a God we thought had abandoned us. Some were bitter at God for condoning the senseless killings. Others refused to believe in God. Where was God's compassion in Treblinka? Many participated only in remembrance of their families, who died *"oyf Kiddush Hashem"* (for the sanctification of His Name). Many were simply grateful to have survived.

In America, my uncles were doing everything possible to bring us to the United States. They not only sponsored us, but they also tried to intercede with several New York politicians to get us there sooner, without success. As soon as it became possible, we registered to immigrate to America. My mother, sick with the flu, went to Naples to get us on the Russian quota, which dictated the number of Russians who were allowed to immigrate to the U.S. She was number 87 on the list. We were lucky to bypass the Polish quota, which numbered in the tens of thousands. It was now a waiting game until our number was called.

The Holocaust Jews in Rome refused to be touched, let alone treated, by Italian doctors. They felt that Italian physicians had inferior medical training and lesser skills. I do not know how these prejudices arose. Nonetheless, the problems of a Jewish population whose health needs went untreated had to be addressed by the Italian authorities for the sake of the larger public welfare. Many Jews were seriously ill and were in desperate need of medical and surgical care. A compromise was reached that allowed my father operating privileges at a major hospital in Rome, provided he limited his care to the Jewish refugees. And so, without an Italian license, my father performed as many as three operations a day. Papa was reimbursed for his services by the Italian government.

With the money he earned, we were able to leave Monte Mario and move into a rented room in Rome proper, on Via de la Giuliana. Our landlady, Signorina Mery, was a kind woman. She did her best to help us adjust to civilian life and became a devoted friend. She was single and lived with her young niece Helena, two years my junior. She introduced us to good Italian food, especially bean dishes such as pasta *fagiole* (bean soup), since meat was still rationed. She also took Helena and me to visit the many tourist sites in Rome, from the Fontana di Trevi to the Vatican. During this time, Papa was busy in the hospital, operating. As long as his ego was being fed by practicing medicine, he acted kinder towards me.

Mama enrolled me in the local elementary school. Wearing the required school uniform made it easier for me to blend in with the other children. Helena tried her best to shelter me from being teased or laughed at. I was enrolled in fourth grade despite the fact that I had never finished first, second, or third grade. Consequently, I was unable to function in the Italian school. I could speak street Italian, and I could read comic books, but that was it. I could not read the schoolbooks, despite our long stay in Italy. Living almost exclusively with Jewish refugees, I was fluent only in Yiddish and Polish. But I knew no Polish grammar, and I certainly could not be expected to be proficient in Italian grammar. I also lacked a basic knowledge of arithmetic, as Papa bypassed teaching arithmetic in favor of algebra.

Predictably, Papa once again reacted with frustration and anger. He was, after all, doing so well as a successful doctor in a new country. Why was I, a mere child, having difficulties? I was proud of Papa for his accomplishments, so why could he not be proud of me? The usual punishments followed. I remember being confined to the room I shared with my parents. It was a particularly beautiful autumn day. I could hear children scurrying, jumping rope, playing ball, playing hopscotch. I brooded over the unfairness of my life, being punished for shortcomings over which I had no control. I was not responsible for the war and the crimes against the Jews, which prevented me from going to school. The war had already robbed me of most of my childhood. So why did peace grant freedom to others but not to me?

My parents hired yet another tutor, this time a college student who treated me with great patience and respect. He taught me Italian history, grammar and spelling, simple arithmetic, and world geography. Despite the lessons, my school performance continued to be marginal. It takes time and diligence to acquire a good foundation of basic knowledge upon which to build, so my first report card brought bad news. As much as I tried, I had years of catching up to do. My father's disgusted reaction was predictable, and Mama did nothing to temper his ire. I suffered in that school for about three months.

In early 1947, quite unexpectedly, we received a letter from the American embassy in Naples informing us we had been granted visas to go to the United States. A giant change in our circumstances was about to unfold; life would never again be the same for us. We were ecstatic.

The Jews of the kibbutz in Monte Mario staged a big farewell for us. One after another, each speaker honored Dr. Chaim Miasnik for his legendary accomplishments during the war. It was an evening of powerful juxtapositions of our two realities. On the one hand, our lives were tied to the events of the past with its memories of death and resistance. On the other hand, we were looking forward to our life in the future with hope in our hearts.

As we waited for a ship to become available in the port of Naples, we packed and got ready to go. My mother bought aluminum pots to take along, as if such pots did not exist in America. I received the phone call that a ship was ready to board in Naples. When my parents returned from the movies, we celebrated the good news. We hired a car to take us to Naples. Signorina Mery insisted that she accompany us as far as the ship, and there we said our final goodbyes.

Our spirits soared. We were going to America! An era was about to end for us. Traveling as refugees across half of Europe, we had reached this moment at last. We had been spared and were now ready to start a permanent new life on a different continent. We had relatives in America who were eagerly awaiting our arrival. I was excited because I was leaving my unhappy experiences in the Italian school. I felt free and alive. My heart was full of hope. Surely life would be different in America, *di goldene medine* (the land of gold).

The vessel that would take us to America, the *Marine Falcon*, was headed for the scrap yard at the end of this journey. Unaware of the ship's fate, we boarded her enthusiastically. As it backed away into the open waters of the Bay of Naples, our eyes clouded over, and the salty ocean spray mixed with our tears. We wept for all those millions of Jews who had perished, including Ala, Tadek, Chana Liba, Ita, and Avram, and so many other relatives and close friends. We were more than ready to leave Europe, to start a new life, in a free nation in a place called Brooklyn, somewhere beyond the horizon. We were no longer just liberated, we were free—free to live—and free to partake of life's bounties and blessings. The haunting presence of our lost loved ones, however, would accompany us through life.

CHAPTER 9
Greenhorns in America

The *Marine Falcon* sailed over the calm waters of the Mediterranean Sea, past the Rock of Gibraltar and into the cold waters of the Atlantic Ocean. As I stared back at the disappearing shoreline of Europe, I wondered what it would be like to live among people who had never experienced war. In America, my father would be a doctor again, and I knew how much that meant to him. My mother would reacquire the closeness of caring siblings to heal her wounds from the loss of her family in Poland. For me, catching up in school and winning the approval of my father were most important. I also wanted new and lasting friend-ships to ease my integration into this new world. But I was fearful that I might never achieve my wishes.

As we sat on the deck of our ship and reminisced about the past, we sang the many Yiddish songs that had accompanied us through life. These songs were like best friends that continued to illuminate the past. Each song resonated with years of cumulative memories of a people reduced to ashes. I sang the songs of the past to charm away my fears of the future. Papa made it clear that

American Jews were naïve about the war and too well off to understand our suffering.

On February 23, 1947, when we sailed past the Statue of Liberty into New York Harbor, we were overwhelmed by the legendary majesty of America. The relatives greeting us were strangers to me. I recognized them from photographs, but I did not think of them as significant people in my life. My family bonds were still tied to Ala and my grandparents. Even while I was surrounded by loving and crying relatives, memories of the past overshadowed the present. My uncles marveled that little Mirele was now so grown, a scrawny, shy, and silent young girl of nearly twelve.

As I looked out the window of the taxi taking us to Brooklyn, I was disappointed by the decaying tenement houses and streets littered with garbage. I was bothered by the lies we had been told—that America was such a rich nation, and that the streets were paved with gold. I wondered why immigrants called America the "land of gold." My child's eyes saw no gold, and if that promise was wrong, then my fears about my future might not be.

The Americans we met struck me as superficial and naïve, chit-chatting on unimportant subjects as if they mattered; their lives, too, seemed ordinary and drab. Conversations seemed trite, almost unworthy of the effort. Our American family, as much as they tried, could not empathize with what we had lived through. While sadly accepting the fact that our relatives had died, they failed to grasp what it meant to have survived: to be the Holocaust's living victims. They were afraid of hearing the near-death experiences we had lived through. In particular, they made ignorant remarks that dismissed my war experiences:

"How lucky you are to have gone through the war as a child."

"Only an adult could fully understand what was going on during the war."

"You were too young to know what was really happening."

"You will soon forget the past; we don't want you to dwell on the war; remember, you are now in America!"

I was aghast. How could Americans assume that I had not fully known Nazi terror? These caring people were, in fact, depriving me of my own feelings and experiences. By not acknowledging my reality, they were looking at me through eyes incapable of seeing.

"It will be easy for you to learn a new language and adjust to a new lifestyle, Mirka," I was assured. In America, close friends and relatives all called me Mirka (my Polish name).

"You are young enough to forget the past. Wait till you go to school and start learning."

The talk of school rubbed new salt into an already deep wound in my psyche. And sooner than I wanted, I was taken to the principal's office of Public School (PS) 225 to register for school. I could not follow any of the conversation because it was all in English, but I did not want to be there under any circumstances. I was terrified as I remembered my agony during the few months I attended school in Rome. Arbitrarily assuming that I had completed fourth grade in Italy, the principal placed me in the second semester of fifth grade. In other words, I was supposed to accomplish five years of elementary education in four months, without knowing any English.

The school interview left me more depressed and anxious than ever. It was in this bad frame of mind that I celebrated my twelfth birthday, knowing that I would be left alone to sink or swim. We could not afford tutors, and I could not count on any meaningful family support because my parents would be too busy getting their own lives settled. In Italy our stay had been temporary; Brooklyn was now our permanent home. I no longer could hope to move away to somewhere new. I no longer could run away from facing my shortcomings and problems.

Showing up in my classroom, I was assigned a desk and given school books, then left to fend for myself without understanding what was being said to me. I sat silent and ashamed. The other students thought I was weird and without a sense of humor. I could hear them laughing at me, and I automatically assumed they disliked me for being "different." The teachers tried to explain things as best they could. They really did not know how to communicate with me, and there were no remedial programs back then. As I withdrew further into my world of inner silence, I became even harder to reach.

When I started another school, PS 100, in the fall of 1948, I was skipped from sixth to seventh grade. My performance, while not especially good, did not reflect the incredible pace at which I was acquiring new knowledge. I had in effect caught up in school and was placed together with children my own age. Even though I was still without friends, I felt less scared because of my increased proficiency in English. I was making major strides in understanding what I was meant to learn.

After my mother's brothers Henry and Morris came to America in the 1920s, they had gone to school and then opened a pharmacy in Brooklyn. Mama began working for them in the pharmacy. She sold ice cream and sodas behind their lunchroom fountain. The twenty-five dollars a week she earned was enough to allow us to rent a place of our own, first a room in a bungalow on Avenue Y, then a small apartment on Neptune Avenue. My father had in the meantime enrolled in courses for foreign doctors to enable him to pass the necessary tests to practice medicine. The tricky part was a prerequisite of having to pass the English Regents exam, a test normally given to all high school graduates, before being allowed to take the New York state medical boards.

This English proficiency exam was especially difficult because it included a large section on American and English literature. Papa had no chance of passing this part of the exam, because he could not read those books, much less understand them. The strategy was to get a perfect score on the English composition part, which totaled 40% of the grade. The word comprehension part was something my father could also study and pass. Papa memorized, down to the last comma, a series of some dozen English compositions so that he could take a given title and regurgitate it verbatim during the test. He failed the exam the first time around, however, and became depressed that he would never pass it. He eventually took it several months later and passed.

Papa began to study and review all the subjects required to pass the New York state medical boards. He teamed up with another Jewish doctor, and together they set up a course of study to fill twelve-hour days. They covered every conceivable specialty, including all the basic and clinical sciences. Some days they worked alone and used the times together to quiz each other. On his first attempt, Papa passed the medical boards and became licensed to practice medicine. He told us a funny anecdote from the exam. He did not know what an "essay" was. The elderly Jewish proctor explained to Papa that an essay was a *maisele* (a little story), so he wrote his answer as a dialogue. Papa then enrolled in a three-month catch-up residency at the Israel Zion Hospital in Brooklyn. His most unusual hospital experience was discovering a patient with typhoid; he had seen hundreds of cases during the war. He reported the finding to the man's doctor but was curtly told to mind his own business. In spite of the brush-off, Papa informed the board of health. A few weeks later, the hospital and the board of health thanked my father for his astute diagnosis, which had prevented a possible hospital crisis. It was a good morale-booster for a man whose entire raison d'être was centered on medicine.

After Papa became licensed, my parents obtained loans from various relatives to get established. They purchased a two-story house on Brighton Second Street in Brooklyn and bought the equipment and supplies needed to outfit a doctor's office. We moved into the house and my father's shingle was hung out in front. Shortly after, my parents Americanized their names; Chaim and Bronka Miasnik became Henry and Betty Mason (the name Mason had also been adopted by my father's brothers when they settled in Pennsylvania many years earlier). My mother stopped working for my uncles, and helped my father run the office instead.

My father's practice grew very quickly. The Jews in the neighborhood sought him out because of his European roots and superior credentials. They appreciated his speaking to them in their own tongue, be it Yiddish, Hebrew, Polish, Russian, German, or in the same poor English that they themselves spoke. He not only provided his patients with outstanding medical care, he also cared about them as people. Dr. Mason was considered to be a real mensch. Many of the older Jews were very poor, and Papa never charged them more than they could afford. Papa was especially kind to the poorest Jews because he understood their hardships in coping with daily life. Quietly and unassumingly, he helped many needy Jews by listening to their financial concerns and then slipping a few dollars into their pockets. Papa kept several small jars in his office, and he filled them with pocket money that he used to help poor Jews in need. Mama and I made believe that we did not know about the jars because the funds were used for a good cause. Many of the Holocaust Survivor doctors who came to New York became established through his generosity.

People who passed our house complimented Papa on his family, as did patients who came from afar. On Sundays some of the refugees from Europe came for special doctor appointments—because they worked during the week, Papa saw them on his day off. They enjoyed recounting to our American family the legendary life my father led during the war. "We remember Dr. Miasnik from so and so," they would say. "Did he tell you what a hero he was in the partisans? We don't know what we would have done without him. We gladly travel from far away to see him. He is so much more caring than any American doctor."

My father's reputation continued to grow in America. He became somewhat of a legend, both in Europe and in America. Although Papa functioned primarily as a general practitioner, in time he was accepted to the staff of two local hospitals, where he began to perform gastro-intestinal surgeries, mainly on the Holocaust survivors in the greater New York City area who had known him in Europe.

Papa had always been a religious man. In time, he joined an Orthodox synagogue. In the early morning, before breakfast, he would go down to his office, put on his *teffilin* (also called *phylacteries, teffilin* are 2 small black leather boxes which contain scrolls inscribed with verses from the Torah), and *daven* (pray). Both my parents became involved in charity and actively participated in several Zionist organizations. They donated thousands of dollars to support

Jews in Israel. Outside of his almost total immersion in medicine, Papa became an avid fan of the Brooklyn Dodgers. He was comical at times, as he tracked different ball games by listening to two portable radios simultaneously.

Life in America was easiest for Mama because she did not have to work for strangers or go to school. She had her two brothers living nearby, about fifteen blocks away. They loved sharing all the details of their daily experiences. As my mother became more involved with her family, the running of my father's office, and *Hadassah*, a women's Zionist organization, she had little time left over for me. Papa was, of course, totally absorbed with his patients, spending all his energies building up his practice and going out on house calls, as he desperately wanted to repay his loans to the family. The togetherness and tightness that we shared as a family in Europe had dissipated in America. Without a common enemy and the goal of surviving at all costs, the bonds between us loosened. Furthermore, I had become a teenager and no longer wanted to be controlled by my parents.

We did, however, always share Holocaust memories among ourselves, as well as with other survivors. We attended yearly gatherings of survivor groups, including survivors of the Lida ghetto, survivors from Warsaw, partisan survivors, Polish Jewish doctors, and other such assemblies. At these events, we jointly sang the many Holocaust songs of the war and Yiddish songs from childhood, as well as familiar Russian and Polish songs. These meetings, journeys of nostalgia, perpetuated the past and made us remember those we lost. It also distinguished us from American Jews, who we felt never really understood us.

Everything in America was new to me: the people, the customs, the foods people ate, the music they listened to. I had never eaten pastrami or corned beef before, even though it was sold in kosher delicatessens. For that matter, I had never eaten bagels and lox before I came to America. Several girls from my school took me for my first trip to a local Chinese restaurant. I looked at the strange menu. Nothing was familiar to me. "How do you know what to order?" I inquired. They laughed at my ignorance and ordered for me.

"What are those wooden sticks at the table?" I said.

"Chopsticks, of course," they replied.

Laughing along with them, I ate my food. Carefully examining my wonton soup, I announced, "Now I understand, wontons are really *kreplach* (dumplings)." As scared as I was of the world around me, I was eager to learn American customs. Adapting to a new culture is not easy. When the conflicts between my past and present became too intense, I withdrew, as always, into silence and isolation.

A group of Jewish girls in my school formed a new social club. I do not really know why I was included, although I was grateful for being asked to join. I was too withdrawn and shy to be more than a spectator. One of the girls called me long and unfamiliar names. She would say, "Miriam, you are a *hypocrite*." I didn't know what a hypocrite was, so I looked up it up in the dictionary. I found that she disliked me because I agreed with everything everyone said or did. I was too insecure to offend anyone by disagreeing and too obedient because of my upbringing. I felt that the group tolerated me but did not really accept me. In January 1949, I graduated from eighth grade at PS 100. I was surprised to have received the PTA award, given to the student who made the most progress in learning. One persistent observation my teachers made to Mama was that I was too melancholy and sad. "She is a very special girl, bright and gifted. She needs to lighten up and smile more," they told her.

Parallel to our outwardly successful adjustments to life in America, an old and concealed family drama raged within our house: my strained relationship with Papa, which had not changed for the better. In spite of the fact that I was often terrified of my father, I loved him for his altruism. While I was proud of his abilities as a doctor, his caring for the poor, and his devotion to people, I wanted him to extend the same kindness to me.

Papa continued to act out his frustrations on me, however, and often in very cruel ways. He could be the most caring and loving dad one moment, then become a bully the next. A plea of "don't tell him" always accompanied my confiding in Mama. I was terrified of how Papa would react to even the most trivial matter. His ire was especially explosive when it came to my school performance. I was catching up in school, but I was doing it too slowly to satisfy him. I was a teenager now, and life was difficult enough for me without having to deal with the temper tantrums that accompanied the arrival of my report cards. His reaction was predictable by now. His face turned red, he yelled, and then he slapped me in a fit of raging anger.

My mother had her own ways of making me feel inadequate. She called me a *paskutstwo* (a really bad person), *leimene hent* (plaster hands, or a clumsy person), and a *shloch* (an untidy or messy person). This further deteriorated my self-esteem, already at an all-time low. I was so depressed most of the time that I never thought to question what my parents said or did. When Mama was angry, she stopped talking to me for days. I remember pleading with her, "Beat me, do anything you want to me, just talk to me." Being called stupid, undeserving, and clumsy was devastating. At times, I wished the war had not ended, so that my parents would love and support me the way they did during the war.

I often backed Mama in her arguments with Papa, only to lose something of value in the process. My mother manipulated me into thinking that she was afraid of my father in order to gain my support in arguments with him. In my efforts to protect my mother, I lost many of my remaining rights in the house. Our house was poorly designed for a doctor's office. The kitchen was in the office area downstairs, and Mama insisted to Papa that they remodel the house and build a new kitchen upstairs, where my bedroom was. They quarreled loud and long, and I feared he would physically hurt her. So I took Mama's side. As a result, I lost my room.

The upstairs now contained the family quarters, while the entire downstairs comprised the doctor's office. A small porch room downstairs in front of the house became my room. It had ten windows and was very cold and drafty in wintertime; it also had no closets. My room was adjacent to the waiting room, and I could hear nearly every word spoken by the patients. This distraction interfered with my homework and my ability to study for exams. I also had no access to a bathroom without going through patient areas. I was relegated to the worst room in the house, evicted from the family living quarters upstairs. Living downstairs also produced the "out-of-sight, out-of-mind" syndrome. In the mornings I got dressed, grabbed a quick slice of bread, and left for school. My mother was still in bed; she never got up to make breakfast or pack a lunch for me. Mirele could take care of herself. The children of other Holocaust survivors were preferentially treated and spoiled; I certainly was not. When we had visitors sleep over, my space always became the floor; Mirele was, after all, accustomed to sleeping on floors.

In February 1949, just shy of my fourteenth birthday, I started ninth grade at Abraham Lincoln High School. I felt lost. Old faces just vanished and were replaced with new ones. Most of the nice Jewish students did not want to have anything to do with me for reasons I could not fully understand. Writing gave me solace and comfort. The pieces I wrote were not the kind that gets entered into diaries; they did not recount reactions to specific events. They were mostly conversations I had with myself and with God. I poured out all the pain in my heart. My body tightened as I wrote about my fears and passions. At times, my migraine headaches turned me into a nonfunctional being, a veritable vegetable. For weeks on end, I lived in a state of deep depression. At times I just wanted to die. I had persistent nightmares stemming from my many fears. I also had fantasies.

One such fantasy was that I would become so sick that I needed an operation that my father would perform. By doing the surgery, he was in fact showing me that he really loved me—he was giving me as much attention as he gave to his sick patients. My best and most powerful day-dreams and fantasies dealt with running away from home and going to live on a kibbutz in Israel. The collective lifestyle of a kibbutz symbolized to me being loved by many people all at once, and no longer feeling alone. In my solitude, my only outlet was through writing.

I started to hang out with a new group of girls in high school who were not the best of students. They aggressively pursued boys anywhere they could find them: in school, at the movies, on the beach, or on the boardwalk. We often walked the boardwalk to Coney Island, met some sailors, and went together on the big roller coasters. The idea was to kiss during our precipitous descents. I was uncomfortable with these activities because I had a difficult time relating to American men. I was attracted to the European Jewish men who I met at the beach in Brighton. These men, mostly in their twenties and thirties, had similar histories to mine. They were more mature, and I had much in common with them. I realized back then that I would eventually wind up marrying a European man, which I did.

My attraction to Holocaust survivors made me realize how much I wanted to immigrate to Israel. In 1948, the War of Liberation for a Jewish homeland in Palestine had been won. I desperately wanted to run away from my life in America and live on a kibbutz, to be with my ilk of Jews. At first, I joined the Zionist youth group *Habonim* ("the builders"), whose function was to recruit and train young Jews for immigration to Israel. I felt elated getting together with the group on weekends and singing and dancing the music of Israel. My experiences there made me feel rooted and secure. I was accepted for what I was and who I was without needing to prove myself. The group met on the other side of Brooklyn, however, too far away to go to alone, so my participation was limited. At times, I daydreamed about running away from home.

My school friends often made me do some of their homework for them. Although my performance at school was still mediocre, I was doing better than they were, and the practice was good for me. Although generally unhappy with my life, I decided that hanging out with friends who didn't treat me very well was better than being home alone. I did not, at first, participate in any school activities, being too shy and withdrawn. Later on, I joined the glee club because I liked to sing. My grades were above average by then, and I began to actually like school, especially the science courses. I registered for two extra summer school science classes. The year I turned fifteen, I read the novel *Arrowsmith* by Sinclair Lewis. It was a thrilling book about the life of a micro-biologist and the exhilaration of scientific discovery. I decided to become a scientist. I would consider the idea of becoming a physician, but only if it entailed research and discovery. Soon, much to my surprise, I was chosen for the school science team.

Though my academic performance had vastly improved, the same could not be said of my social adjustments. This became apparent at the next big event, my Sweet Sixteen party, which my friends threw for me at my home. While it was supposed to be my coming of age, it depressed me terribly. The boy who was supposed to be my date was a jerk, and I heard the others whispering about me and laughing at me. Perhaps I had become paranoid; I was certainly insecure. I could not wait for everyone to leave. That night, I crawled under my desk and cried most of that night. I hated myself. I hated my friends. I hated life.

My mother signed me up at the Arthur Murray dance studio so that I could learn to dance. I hoped the training would make me feel less physically awkward. I was very shy and had problems relating to boys. I attended several parties where I was made to feel humiliated and isolated by criticism and laughter. I remember coming home in tears after one of these disastrous evenings, only to find my father angry with me for a reason I can't recall. I could stand it no longer. I went to the bathroom, and while there, I stared at the iodine bottle with its skull and crossbones. I stood mesmerized and calm. I thought back over my past and present life and I decided that I had suffered enough. I was alone, with no real friends or allies, devoid of love and support, in too much pain to go on. I was finally going to hurt my father for the rest of his life. I could not tell him how angry I was at him, so I was going to express my inner rage by killing myself. My mother would never forgive him if I died. It seemed for the moment the poetic and perfect end to all my problems. Fortunately, I had second thoughts almost immediately, and I didn't take the poison.

In the summer, I worked as an assistant in my father's office. We were finally at peace, my father and I. He had become more considerate of me, and he treated me with respect. He wanted to pay me more than what we had originally agreed. He often sent me to the beach. He thought that I needed time to relax. I had made it. I had won. My father was giving up his control over me. I had grown up. He was actually telling people that I was smart and accomplished. I was happy to experience this softness from him, the same kind-ness he routinely offered to strangers. I enjoyed a sense of freedom. He became a loving and devoted father who enjoyed doting on me and taking pride in all my accomplishments.

I graduated high school in June 1952, at seventeen. My grades were good enough for me to be accepted into New York University (NYU). I had struggled hard for this accomplishment, my entry to adulthood. Graduation meant a new life for me, the start of a process of discovery and transformation. My grief had sharpened my senses, my energies became more focused. The years of crying had washed away many of my fears and painful memories and exposed new paths for me to follow.

Five years after coming to the United States, we became American citizens. I finally understood the meaning of the phrases that eluded me earlier. America was indeed the "land of gold" that I had been promised so long ago, a nation like no other; a place where each person could pursue his dreams and reach his greatest potential.

In September 1952, although still living at home, I started attending NYU. For the first time, I was looking forward to going to school. I hoped that the knowledge I would acquire in college would help me overcome the excessive sense of inadequacy I still felt. Freedom was scary but at the same time exhilarating. I had dreams. I noticed that I was becoming younger and more spirited as I grew chronologically older. I had learned how to laugh at myself. I was breaking free of the chains that kept me trapped and depressed for

most of my childhood. What a joy to live without being the prey of life, to have the opportunity to become
my own master. My goals, as lofty as those of *Arrowsmith*, directed me to major in science. I was a pre-med student headed for a career in medical research.

Like a bud in springtime programmed to bloom in response to the rain and warm sun, I was opening up to an entire new world—a world of philosophies and of ideas, of art and science, of music and language. I enrolled in an introductory art course that was taught inside the many museums in New York City. Sometimes we visited the private studios of well-known artists and sculptors. The thrill of seeing original works of art made a powerful and lasting impression on me. I fell in love with the works of the French Impressionists; I also discovered the Cubists and the Expressionists. I began to dream that some-day I too would be able to express my feelings through art. From then on, art became a passion in my life, one that would only intensify with time and experience, one that would give me sustenance and feed my spirit.

Many of the other women I met in college lacked a sense of professional commitment. They were content to approach the future with resignation that no matter their academic accomplishments, they'd ultimately become wives and mothers.

There had to be more to life, I thought. While I wanted a husband and children, I also wanted something else, whatever that something was. Years later, when I read Betty Friedan's *The Feminine Mystique*, I found that she described the desire for more out of life than was found in many of the college women of those days.

A cousin, also called Miriam, was eager to introduce me to a young man she had known for many years, dating all the way back to before the war, when she lived in Paris. She described him as a brilliant young physicist. Henry Brysk called me when he visited his parents in the Bronx in December 1953. He asked me out to a chamber music concert. Henry was short, with curly brown hair, blue eyes, pleasant smile, and a bad case of acne. He was shy and spoke very slowly, thinking over the exact wording of each sentence before verbalizing it. This was no ordinary man. Henry was an intellectual with a physics Ph.D. from Duke University; he was now an assistant professor at Vanderbilt University. I was awed and overwhelmed by his credentials. While he had no detectable foreign accent, he was definitely European in his mannerisms.

Henry and his brother Marcel had come to America as children in April 1941. Henry's parents, Srulik and Sarah Brysk, were avid members of the *Bund*, the Jewish Socialist movement that advocated a secular Yiddish cultural autonomy for Eastern European Jewry. Originally from Poland, they had moved to Paris in 1923 because of persecution due to Srulik's union activities. The family escaped from Paris just ahead of the Nazi occupation, moving to southern France, which was ruled by the Nazi-sponsored Vichy government. The American Federation of Labor helped them to emigrate to the U.S. via Portugal. The garment unions in New York (some of whose leaders Srulik had known in his youth in Poland) secured an apartment and a job for him. Srulik resumed his trade as a cap maker in lower Manhattan.

At the chamber music concert Henry and I attended, a *countertenor* (a classical male singer whose voice is in the low soprano range) sang Elizabethan songs. This type of music was totally new to me. The only classical music I was familiar with was Italian opera. Afterwards, Henry asked about my views and opinions on all sorts of different subjects. I was overwhelmed; no one had ever cared to know in detail my intellectual views on worldly matters. I remember holding his hand. He had such well-formed, gentle hands. I felt secure and satisfied. Henry was a mature and educated European—as well as a Holocaust survivor.

By the time Henry called for another date, however, I felt less sure of myself. I was concerned that I was not intelligent enough for a man of his caliber, and the educational discrepancy between us was intimidating. Henry had graduated from high school at fifteen, earned a bachelor of science degree from City College, a master's degree from the University of Pennsylvania a year later, and a Ph.D. in theoretical physics from Duke University two years after that, on his twenty-third birthday. He knew himself, and where he was headed in life. I only had dreams of being a scientist someday. Going out with Henry was an intellectual challenge; it scared me. Still, I liked him precisely because he *was* a challenge! With time, as I thought more about Henry and compared him to the other men in my life, I realized that I was in fact attracted by his European roots and his awesome intellect. In spite of my perceived lack of education, Henry believed in me. He was convinced that I had the potential to learn and excel.

We began writing to each other. The letters he sent did not make it easy to maintain a viable relationship. He wanted to discover what was in my brain. I, on the other hand, wanted to know what was in his heart. No matter what I wrote, I could not get him to express his feelings or passions. While it is interesting to read an encyclopedia, it is not something you would cuddle up to on a cold, rainy evening! I was also bothered by his lack of belief in God, not that I had any religious education. The Bundists did not believe in God. They sought also to distance themselves from Israel, and they condemned its destruction of European Yiddish culture and language. For me as a Zionist, Israel was a miracle that took the Holocaust for the world to establish. This was the place I wanted to live. This issue divided us for many years.

In spite of all my reservations, however, I found myself falling in love with Henry. I liked his shyness and his social awkwardness, qualities that also described me. I was pleased that he thought I was intelligent. He wanted me to continue my education as far as I possibly could. In those days, when many men demanded that their women dream of nothing more than sitting home and raising families, Henry's opinions were revolu-tionary. Years later, I asked him what he thought of me in those days. Smiling, he said that unlike other women he had met, I had a thirst for knowledge and for life, together with an insatiable curiosity—rare qualities among women of those days, whose ultimate goal, whether they had a college education or not, usually focused on marriage and children.

While Papa had also encouraged me to have a career, I did not want to become a physician; I wanted to become a scientist. I needed a clean break from my father, yet I was terrified at confronting him on this issue. Despite my adulthood and the changes in the dynamics of our relationship, I still continued to be afraid of Papa. I hesitantly informed him that I was not going to apply to medical school, and that I wanted to become a scientist and get a graduate degree instead. He turned that familiar shade of red. "Don't you realize that as a physician you will become someone important?" he implored. "People will respect you. You will be your own boss. As a scientist you will always have a boss over you telling you what to do."

"That is not my basis for wanting to become a scientist," I replied. "Science suits my interests better."

"Don't you realize that we would have never survived the war had I not been a medical doctor?"

"The war is long over, Papa."

"You will be sorry for your decision for the rest of your life. Life will punish you for it."

Henry's letters acquired a more personal and loving tone. In December 1954, he came to New York to attend a meeting of the American Physical Society. He told me how much he loved me and asked me to marry him. We sat that cold night in the parked car, speaking of love, of deep inner feelings, and of plans to marry in June. I wandered around that spring with a twinkle in my eye, happy to have found a man I felt safe with.

Henry had just accepted a new position at the radiation laboratory in the Electrical Engineering Department of the University of Michigan. I inquired at the university whether I could finish my undergraduate schooling there. They informed me that I had to spend two years in residence to do so. With only eighteen credits left to graduate, I decided to remain in New York and take those credits over the course of the summer—a Herculean task, but I was confident that I could do it.

At the age of twenty, in 1955, I graduated from NYU. Completely washed out and exhausted, I heaved a big sigh of relief. It had taken eight long years of struggle in American schools to reach this point—eight years—exactly equivalent to the number of years I had spent as a child in Europe during the Holocaust and its aftermath. I took note of how much I had matured. I was no longer living in fear of being separated from my parents in the Lida ghetto. I was no longer the quiet, scrawny young girl with sad dark eyes, unable to speak English. And I was no longer in fear of my next report card—afraid my father would violently disapprove of my poor performance. Most importantly, my painful past did not hinder me from having dreams and living them to their fruition.

Henry and I married in June 1955, in Brooklyn. The ceremony was touching; the rabbi spoke of the miracle of a Jewish child surviving the Holocaust. I noticed that all of our family and many of the guests were in tears. People kept congratulating me, reminding me of our tragic past. I thought back to my Aunt Ala and my grandparents and how much joy it would have brought them to have participated in my wedding. There was much to celebrate: A child of the Holocaust was spared to propagate life. Within her were the seeds to carry on the lifeblood of Judaism.

Immediately after our honeymoon in Maine, Henry started working at the University of Michigan in Ann Arbor while I began taking the 18 summer school credits in order to graduate in September. Henry came when I had finished and we drove to Ann Arbor. We finally were able to begin our life together—and plan for the future.

EPILOGUE

Our two daughters, Judy and Havi, were born in 1957 and 1959, respectively. Concurrently, I obtained my Master of Science degree in bacteriology from the University of Michigan. To the great joy of our families, we moved back to the New York area, bringing with us two delightful children for them to savor. While I adored my children, staying home day after day as a wife and mother became depressing after a while. Surely, there had to be more to life, I thought. My first venture out of the house was a part-time position as lecturer in a microbiology course at Queens College. Henry insisted that in order to teach at the college level I needed a Ph.D. As a result, when Havi turned three, I returned to graduate school, first to St. John's University for one year, then to Columbia University. I was driven to pursue my dream of becoming a scientist. Nothing could stop me, not even long commutes, first from Long Island, then from Westchester, all the way to upper Manhattan. My parents had tried to dissuade me from pursuing my folly. Surely, as a mother with young children, my place was at home caring for my family. How attitudes change: it was no longer my father who demanded excellence from me—I now demanded it from myself. A powerful surge of adrenalin traversed my spirit, as if a long dormant seed had suddenly sprouted; I felt alive again.

I earned my Ph.D. from Columbia University's Biological Sciences Department. My research in bacterial physiology focused on how bacteria both produce and metabolize cyanide. The work was esoteric enough to suit my taste—I felt like a detective, and enjoyed the challenge. In fact, at the age of thirty-two, my friends started referring to me as "Agatha" Brysk, in honor of my favorite literary detective, Agatha Christie. After my successful thesis defense, my family, particularly my father, was elated and proud of me.

There followed three post-doctoral fellowships. The first at the Institute of Muscle Disease in New York was a continuation of my research on cyanide metabolism in bacteria, during which I discovered a new cyan amino acid. The work was published in record time by the Journal of Biological Chemistry. Then Henry took a position in San Diego and we moved to California. My boss at the University of California in San Diego, where I worked next, informed me even before I started work that as a woman, I had no future in academia. In keeping with his belief, he treated me not as a scientist but as a technician. I investigated how plants cells synthesize their cell walls. Because of my boss's attitudes, my work environment became progressively worse.

Exhausted and demoralized after two years, I fell into a three-year-long depression which kept me home, believing I did not have what it took to be a scientist. With no self-confidence, I was afraid to look for another job. During this period we moved back to Ann Arbor, because Henry's company moved from San Diego to Michigan. I desperately needed a shrink who would help me redeem my self-confidence, but back then it was not the thing to do. So as my own form of therapy, I set up a darkroom at home and began to experiment with alternative photography, making color images from black-and-white negatives. By then my daughters were in high school.

I eventually returned to work. My fellowship at the University of Michigan in the mid-1970s focused on the biochemistry of skin and epidermal differentiation. From among the available fellowships, I chose to work with skin, reasoning that the research would enable me to obtain a future academic appointment in a dermatology department. I applied to the National Institutes of Health (NIH) and was awarded a fellowship of my own to pursue a research project on basal cell carcinoma.

During this period my father suffered two consecutive heart attacks. While his physical recovery exceeded expectations (he resumed work after two months), his mental faculties began to deteriorate, and he was manifesting major memory lapses. He would answer calls from patients without knowing with whom he was speaking. Alarmed at the possible malpractice implications, my mother forced him to retire, and they moved to a condominium in Florida. Once in North Miami Beach, alone among a sea of other Jewish retirees, my parents' lives began to unravel. The Zionist organizations in Florida were not interested in their participation, only in their monetary contributions. My father's memory continued to deteriorate, and he lost interest in both baseball and medicine. In time, the only thing he remembered from his years as a doctor was how to take a pulse.

As his memory reverted to the time we first came to America, he became agitated and guilt-ridden. His mind became fixated on our early years in America and our adversarial relationship. During a Passover visit I made to Florida, he approached me in tears, begging, "Mirele, forgive me." I put my arms around him and, with tears in my own eyes, I forgave him and told him how much I loved him, and how much it meant to me to have finally reached this reconciliation. As I set his conscience free, he became more calm and content. My mother died in 1987 from cancer, and my father two years later from Alzheimer's disease. The suffering and deaths of my parents were two of the most stressful and depressing events of my life.

Henry's boss in Ann Arbor died while testifying before a congressional committee in Washington on the importance of developing laser fusion as an energy source. To fill the void that followed, Henry accepted a position to continue this research at the Los Alamos National Laboratory in New Mexico. I followed him later, after obtaining an appointment as research assistant professor of dermatology and biochemistry at the Medical School of the University of New Mexico. By then, our daughter Judy was attending the six-year medical program at the University of Michigan and was married to another medical student in the program. Havi had graduated from high school and was starting college at the University of Michigan.

While in Albuquerque, I applied for and was awarded my first NIH grant to work on cell surface glycoprotein changes of skin cells as they undergo differentiation. The dean at the medical school was uncooperative in helping the dermatology department establish a research laboratory of its own. That impelled my boss, Dr. Edgar (Ben) Smith to leave the University of New Mexico to become chair of dermatology at the University of Texas Medical Branch in Galveston (UTMB). He asked me to come with him to set up a research laboratory. I accepted his offer of a tenure-track position, and I moved to Texas in July 1979. In the meantime, Henry moved to

Virginia to become a visiting professor of physics at Virginia Tech. We were apart for a year and a half; in early 1981 Henry moved to Texas and worked for an oil company. I was elated with my new position. I arrived at UTMB with a newly-funded NIH grant, and I was given seed money to set up a lab of my own. In addition to my position in the department of dermatology, I was awarded joint appointments in the departments of micro-biology and of biochemistry. I was supposedly living my dream.

A year later, however, I experienced the onset of an especially severe depression that had prompted me to bring home my cyanide bottle from the lab. I had reached a low from which I could no longer extricate myself. In desperation, I began to examine my life. In doing so, I realized how tough my childhood and later life had been. Throughout my life, I have had a stubborn determination and persistence to go on even when deprived of a reason for doing so. I clung to hopes with the tenacity I learned surviving the Holocaust. Tenacity is a noble attribute; however, it brings no joy. I realized that I would never experience joy as long as I was dealing with my persistent bouts of depression, feelings of worthlessness, inadequacy, and anxiety from years of being thought of as stupid. Clearly, I needed to gain perspective on the issues that prevented me from healing and experiencing inner peace. I decided to begin psychotherapy, and thus began a long and painful journey lasting many years. I was fortunate to work under the guidance of a tough woman therapist who made me confront all my demons. This was also a period of incredible personal and professional growth that transformed how I viewed and lived life. I replaced my feelings of worthlessness with those of confidence and empowerment.

Despite my personal struggles, I continued to achieve professionally. I was promoted to associate professor with tenure in 1982, and in 1988, promoted to full professor in three departments (dermatology, microbiology and biochemistry). In a department that had no previous research operation, I literally had to build a laboratory from scratch, scrounging space and then gradually accumulating test tubes, chemicals, equipment and other materials. Slowly, I began the most creative journey I had ever travelled. For years I had only dreamed of being an independent scientist doing my own research, and now I was actually doing it—and publishing my results. In the late 1980s, my department moved to a newly renovated building. As a reward for my research contributions, I was allowed to design a new spacious laboratory that was claimed to be the most custom-built on campus and the envy of many scientists.

When I retired in December 1999, I left behind

a well-equipped facility with over a million dollars' worth of equipment. The laboratory had been a one-woman operation, apart from support staff. Its scope was extended by collaborations with faculty from other departments with their own laboratories, principally Dr. Srinivasan Rajaraman (Pathology) and Drs. Istvan Arany and Stephen Tyring (Microbiology). Dr. Toshio Horikoshi spent over a year in my laboratory and then continued his research in Japan as we collaborated even after my retirement. My laboratory was mostly funded by several grants from the National Institutes of Health, supplemented by grants from the Welch Foundation, from companies (S.C. Johnson, Kanebo), and by institutional funds.

My research focused on epidermal biology. Most of it was directed at elucidating the molecular mechanisms by which normal skin sheds and how the shedding process becomes altered in skin diseases such as psoriasis and cancer. The cells in the outer skin undergo a continual process of cell replacement known as *epidermal differentiation*. The aim of this process is to create an outer layer of dead cells, which acts as a protective barrier to the living cells beneath. I was the first to show that *glycoproteins* (proteins with attached sugar complexes) were present in the outer dead cell layer. I inventoried these molecules and traced changes in their abundance in diseased skin as compared to normal skin. I also discovered and characterized previously unidentified molecules that are critical to the normal shedding process of the outer skin. One of these molecules acts like a "super glue," holding together the dead cells. It is absent in psoriasis, where shedding is abnormal. This molecule has enzymatic activity; I characterized its functions and cloned its DNA structure.

In collaborative studies with scientists from microbiology, we were able to correlate the levels of modulators of immunity (such as interferon) with the stage of cell differentiation in tumors as compared to normal skin, elucidating aspects of tumor biology. As most of my experiments used cultured cells, I began to develop new methods for culturing difficult-to-grow cells. For a long time, I had been interested in the biology of basal cell carcinoma of the skin; however, this tumor had resisted being grown in culture. Using a new approach, I was the first to grow tumor cells from basal cell carcinoma in culture, thus facilitating the study of this most prevalent cancer.

While most of my investigations were in basic research, I also ventured into areas of direct clinical application. I developed new methodologies for growing and grafting skin cells at a stage in their life cycle when they are capable of cell division (and hence create grafts that renew and survive indefinitely), ultimately obtaining two patents. In collaboration with the clinical faculty in dermatology, I was able to culture enough cells from tiny biopsies of a patient's normal skin to graft large leg ulcers and lesions on burn patients. In one instance, a wheelchair-bound man in his late seventies with a large ulcer received a graft from my laboratory; he healed quickly and was able to dance at his wedding. I derived much satisfaction from working with patients directly and helping their non-healing wounds heal. Using the same techniques, I grew and grafted epidermal pigment cells as a treatment for *vitiligo* (a skin pigmentation disorder in which the skin becomes mottled with white patches). After the work was published, it was mentioned in *Prevention*, triggering calls from mothers from as far away as Australia seeking treatment for their children.

Several years ago, the dermatology department was undergoing an external review for which I wrote up the background on research. Face to face and alone with the five reviewers who praised my role in the department, I commented, "I guess that's not bad for a Holocaust survivor." The chairman of the committee smiled at me and said, "Miriam, you haven't just survived, you have triumphed."

I used the knowledge and wisdom I had gained from my academic and life experiences to champion the development of women in academia. Upon being tenured, I resolved to become involved in the major activities of the medical school. I joined and influenced the deliberations of vital committees, and became a good citizen of the institution. I campaigned to enable junior women faculty to receive funding from intramural grants, become appointed to university committees, and earn promotions and tenure. With time and experience, I became a mentor. I advised numerous faculty women on issues vital to their career development: writing a good curriculum vitae (CV), bargaining with a chairman for promotions and raises, becoming politically active, and most importantly, saying no when asked to undertake menial jobs that often hinder academic growth. I encouraged them to focus their activities in ways that would benefit their own professional development. I also reached out to them in friendship, caring for them as people, sensitive to their desire to balance career and family obligations.

Henry had retired in the mid-1990s, and stayed home waiting for me to retire. I invited him to come and work in my lab, saying that my lab was now our family business, and I wanted him to help me run it. He did the bookkeeping and paperwork on the grants. He helped me write manuscripts for publication and new grant applications. We wrote 23 published research manuscripts together, and I proudly put his name on all of them; we were now the Drs. Brysk.

I retired from UTMB in December 2000. Funding for running my laboratory was becoming progressively harder to obtain. I was spending most of my time writing new grant applications, instead of doing the research itself. My teaching load had vastly increased, after a revision of our medical school curriculum made me a director in the dermatology/hematology/musculoskeletal course. My creative juices were wearing down, and my activities often felt repetitive. Although I had amassed a CV of some thirty pages, and over eighty publications, I no longer felt productive. I wanted to focus my energies on things that now mattered more to me. I felt a need to complete my memoir, and to devote more time to art. We also wanted to live closer to our children and grandchildren in Michigan and become more a part of their lives. So in May 2001, we moved back to Ann Arbor and I began yet another new and creative phase of my life.

My daughter Judith Brysk, M.D., is a gynecologist in private practice; she is married to Douglas Elbinger, a former photographer, and now Energy Policy Analyst in the Detroit area. She has three children: twin boys Benjamin and Joshua, born in 1980, and daughter Hannah, born in 1989. My daughter Havi Mandell, M.S.W. and Ph.D. is a clinical psychologist and holistic healer. She has a son, David, born in 1983, and a daughter, Sarah, born in 1985. Being together again with my family in Michigan has given Henry and me enormous pleasure and joy.

Throughout my professional life, beginning with the art appreciation course I took at NYU, I have had an ongoing interest in expressing my feelings through art. For me, art is more than a portrayal of images; it is an outward expression of an inner need that cannot be otherwise realized. My art, like my life, has been strongly influenced by my childhood experiences in the Holocaust. My first venture into art was through black-and-white photography, after I purchased my first camera in 1968. Through the starkness of black-and-white photography, I searched for the emotions expressed in human faces and in the language of their bodies. Next, I manipulated black-and-white negatives; I copied the images on successive high-contrast film, and then recombined the images through colored filters and beam splitters to create impressionistic paintings. My acrylic paintings in the 1980s depicted the raw pain of my childhood experiences, as I was reliving them through psychotherapy. As my soul was healing, color became central to my work. In time, I acquired a strong need to express myself using the full spectrum of bright and vivid colors. I tried to project life's flow, celebration, and continuity; the joy in my life was reflected in my art.

In the late 1990s, the computer became vital to my work. Using several graphic programs, I created original images on the computer; the computer monitor had become my canvas. Some works were painted directly on the computer, some were derived through the manipulation of algorithmic equations, and still others were derived from digital photographs. After living my dream of being a scientist, I am finally living another, that of being an artist.

After moving to Ann Arbor in 2001, I joined a group of local digital artists who helped me hone my graphic skills on the computer. My renewed artistic interest in the Holocaust was fueled by my return in 2002 to the former locations of the ghettos and camps of Eastern Europe. I cried my way through the entire trip as the gaping wounds of my past reopened. I allowed the pain of those memories to again be felt, as I remembered those of my own family who perished. Throughout the trip, I was haunted by images of my vanished family, while childhood fears reemerged as frightening nightmares. My entire being was shaking in horror as I sobbed for the six million of my people who had so inhumanly and painfully perished. I felt a deep need to portray their suffering and return to them their dignity as Jews.

When I returned home, I felt fully primed to write my story and to portray the suffering of my people through art. What followed over the next several years were my memoir—*Amidst the Shadows of Trees* in 2007—and two large bodies of art—*In a Confined Silence* in 2005 and *Children of the Holocaust* in 2008. I have since had some 25 solo art exhibits and several of my works are now in the permanent art collection at Yad Vashem.

To recreate memory through art, I chose photographs of actual Jews who perished, including those of my own family. I use images of real victims individually, so as to personalize the Holocaust. While the Germans wanted to dehumanize the Jews, I want to reverse that process and remember one victim at a time, not just a gigantic number—six million. I wanted to retain the fidelity of each face with minimal distortion, tell that person's story and put that art in historical context.

Wherever I have displayed my art, people have commented on how much they had learned of the Holocaust from my presentations and how moved they were by the images. They urged me to write an art book. As I pondered the idea further, I realized that such a book would make a powerful teaching tool for college and high school students that would allow them to personalize the Holocaust by identifying with the experiences of individual victims.

The book—*"The Stones Weep: Teaching the Holocaust through a Survivor's Art"*—was completed in 2012; it includes a section written by my co-author Margaret Lincoln on lesson plans for using the art to teach the Holocaust to high school students. It is a unique book for transmitting the complexity of this dark period in history in an accessible and meaningful way; the art engages the emotions while the captions deliver the historical context.

I have recently begun working on a new exhibit of Holocaust art—*The Scroll of Remembrance.* Unlike my previous art, which focused on the plight of individual Jews, this one portrays the fate of Jewish communities under German rule. I am grateful that in my late seventies, my creative juices still continue to flow, and allow me to perpetuate the memory of the massacred six million innocent European Jews whose lives were so tragically terminated. In my strong identification with the victims, I have sought to ensure in my own way that they did not suffer a double death—dying in the Holocaust and then dying again by being forgotten.

I also want to express the joy I now feel, to have survived the Holocaust, to have been blessed with a loving family—my husband Henry, daughters Judy and Havi, and five wonderful grandchildren, and to have had the opportunity to live a full and creative life, on my own terms, as a passionate individualist.

EULOGY FOR PAPA

*(Written in October 1989
by Judy, Havi, and Me)*

I look at you now and view you for the very last time, yet you will always be in my thoughts and memory. You are now together with your parents, Chenoch and Chana Liba, and with your beloved Broneczka. And I know that God has taken you back to Him, with arms open, saying, "This was a special man that I created, a real mensch."

To know you is to go back to your place of birth in Lida and to your heritage and upbringing. Chana Liba, your mother, had endowed and empowered you with a tradition that stemmed from having been a descendant of the Tzaddikim. You were indeed a son of Chana Liba and all those traditions that were the most noble and holy for our people: warmth, devotion, humility, giving, caring, and healing. I remember your recounting to me of how you sat in the woods outside Lida reading the poetry of Bialik, how in your heart you were among the original *Chalutzim*. Your favorite was "To a Bird"—you yearned for freedom for the Jews just as the bird that flew free. You burned with your love for Eretz Israel.

Your mother told you to acquire a trade and go

out into the world and serve. You would often recount how she told you that a man is given two names in life—the first name is the one by which he is called, the last name he must earn. Surrounded by anti-Semites, you became a physician, and later settled in Warsaw. There you became a surgeon and a healer and earned your last name. Serving the very poor and those who often could not pay, you were called the "King of the Poor." There you also met Broneczka and there your only child Mirele was born.

In 1939 the war began and forever changed how our lives were to be lived. You were to be tested to your fullest: to find a way to survive and to retain your gentle humanity among beasts; to be a healer among murderers; and to be a mensch amidst the brutality and death that surrounded and devoured us. It was a war in which the burning bush of our people was almost totally consumed in the gas chambers and ovens of Auschwitz, Majdanek, and Treblinka. Those in our own ghetto in Lida were nearly totally slaughtered in one single day. I remember how you looked at me as we were selected to die, but were spared at the end because you were still needed as a doctor.

A group of Jewish partisans came to the ghetto to take us out into the virgin forests of White Russia, for they needed a skilled surgeon. There, on a small island with a hospital surrounded by swamps, you made your very finest contribution of saving lives, of not only the hopelessly wounded, but also of the many unarmed Jews, families of older Jews, Jewish women and children who had no one to feed and protect them. How many times you placed your own life at stake to save those innocents when they were falsely accused by the anti-Semites around us. You were awarded by the Russians in Moscow the prestigious Orden Lenina for your work in the partisans.

I remember our lives in Monte Mario, Italy, as refugees after the war. You circumcised one of the first children to have been born to Holocaust survivors. You chanted the very first High Holiday services with your heart full. By special dispensation from the Italian government, you were able to operate on and heal the surviving remnants of our people. There was hardly anyone who had not heard of Dr. Chaim Noach Miasnik, his deeds were a legend even back then.

I remember when we came to America and were reunited with our family here. You built a new life for us. As Dr. Henry Mason in Brighton Beach, you also became a legend. You truly cared for people with an open hand and a loving heart. You ferreted away "knippel money" in your medical books in your office for the purpose of helping a patient in need. You never expected to be paid back, but were happy for the person who could.

You were a central figure in the community. You walked every morning and evening through the neighborhood greeting those you met. The rabbi would stop by your front porch on Saturdays, the fruit vendors would put aside their best fruit for you, and your patients would stop to share family news or thank you for your care. You were especially proud when walking with your family on the boardwalk or down the avenue as if they were your greatest accomplishment. Those who knew you will never forget you, your kindness, your devotion, and your love.

You were a man who enjoyed the simple joys of life—who had music in his soul. You were always humming the Yiddish songs of your childhood, the *partizaner lieder*, songs of Israel, folk songs, and bits of opera. You were a religious man. You supported your schul and felt pride in continuing the traditions of your people. You treasured the holidays, celebrating them joyously. I remember you singing all the songs and prayers at the Pesach (Passover) seders with Henry, Morris, and Sevek, reveling in freedom in honor of the Jews who did survive to participate in their own seders.

Who were you, Chaim Noach?

A mensch, symbolizing the very best in your people. You dealt with people in a loving and giving tradition. You did not need to receive credit for all the people you helped out; a Jew, caring for our people and our traditions. There was a sense of God when you davened daily wearing teffilin.

A man of holiness; God Himself was proud at this man He had created.

An ardent Zionist and lover of Israel, always giving and helping to support our eternal homeland.

A hero of our people; your picture hangs in Israel at the Museum of the Kibbutz of Jewish Partisans.

A doctor and a healer. Money did not matter; you treated and operated on all those who were sick.

Husband to your beloved Broneczka; you were always together giving fully to each other and living the best traditions of our people.

My father. How you loved your Mirele; and how you taught me the values of life; and how proud you were of my accomplishments.

A grandfather to Judy and Havi. You would indeed be proud of the very unique and special people that they are today, their values, their menschlichkeit, and their accomplishments.

A great grandfather to Benjamin, Joshua, David, and Sarah, and our little one about to be born (Hannah).

All those that are here for this service: your lives were all touched by having known him as a relative or as a friend. *Tatele*, God has always walked with you, and now, you yourself are walking with God.

POEMS

Reflections at a Yiddish Song Concert

Songs of a people who no longer know
    the words
A culture now reduced to transliterations
This the final legacy of Hitler's survivors
Threads of melodies still touching hearts
Of grandchildren scattered over
    continents
I sit here with eyes glazed over in silent
    tears
Remembering the many times I sang
    these songs
In shabby houses of the Lida Ghetto
In virgin forests of White Russia
In DP camps of postwar Europe
At New York meetings of war survivors
Staring at my pa's glazed eyes
Now remembering his own parents
They too once sang these haunting
    melodies
Raisins and Almonds, Tumbalalaika—
A culture and traditions now gone forever
A vanishing world whose heart and soul
Was gassed and burned in Auschwitz and
    Treblinka

All that remains are memories
Of another time, another age, another
    place
But memories too are tangible and real
As a survivor I feel like a messenger who
Still remembers both tunes and words
My children still know the songs of
What are now only Xerox copies of the
    past

Your Song

(In memory of my mother)

Endless horizons of snow-covered forests
Winds and wolves howling in the night
Leech-laden swamps frozen and still
All life forms hidden in hibernation
No other moving creatures but us
Our frigid bodies hovering and shivering
Sharing the warmth still left in our veins
No food to eat, no water to drink
Snow our only sustenance
Moving from one cold place to another
Jews are fleeing to escape their fate
Not to be discovered, not to be
    surrounded
Not to be captured, not to be slaughtered
Papa is gone to where I don't know
My only companion unable to protect me
Her body sick, delirious with disease
Her fever rising, no pulse to the touch
Mamele, mamele, please don't die
Please don't leave me in this place all
    alone
Who'll be left to warm me, who to love me
I cry and I mourn your imminent loss
Doomed to my own death by
    abandonment

No one in this world can possibly know
The frightening terror of being left alone
God can you hear my silent inner cries
Do you still listen to your children that
    are lost
Suddenly, miraculously you open your
    eyes
You're alive!
God has heard me!
You have survived
I held you and kissed you, eyes red from
    crying
You turned my way and to my surprise
You sang your favorite Polish love song
More tears of joy stream down my face
I am no more an orphan, I have my mama
I knew that this moment would always be
    with me
Inscribed there forever in my heart and
    my soul
How many times since, wherever we
    were
Whenever, wherever you sang this your
    song
I would hold you and cry and remember
    those days
Of times of great gladness, of times of
    thanksgiving
Of survival and of faith, of life and of
    hope

You're gone now, but I still sing your
    song
I think of the transient nature of life
Of being young, of growing old
Of children, of grandchildren
Of saying Kaddish
And goodbye forever

The Parting

(Separation from my parents
in the Lida ghetto)

Birds flying freely in the hot days of
    August
Wheat fields and sunflowers ripe for the
    harvest
Animals napping under shadows of shade
    trees
Lazy summer days to rest in, and dream
    in
So remote are these scenes from our own
    existence
Overwhelming stark contrasts of not
    having, of not being

Jews caged in ghettos enclosed by barbed
    wires
Helpless and hopeless their wretched
    hungry lives
Enduring their misery in a confined silence
Killing fields demanding their daily
    human quotas
For slaughtering pits from which no one
    returned
What next God? Our children their next
    victims

All Jewish children to be murdered!
My mother and father in a desperate
  frenzy
Where can we hide you, Mirele, our
  child?
I'm to be taken to a farm of a peasant
  woman
Whose child my father had rescued from
  death

And so it came to pass that we stood
  there together
At the crossroads of where our paths were
  to part
Not knowing we'll ever see each other
  again
Last hugs and kisses and final good
  byes
Hearing the anguished voices of my
  parents
With final instructions for my new way of
  life
"Never say where you come from,
Do exactly as you're told,
Play with the children,
Pretend you're a Christian,
Speak only Polish,
Never speak Yiddish,
From today on you're no longer a Jew
May God go with you, Mirele."

A stranger had come to take me away
To an alien life in an unknown place
How could he possibly know how I felt?
Unexpressed fears cradled within me
Unuttered words choking my breathing
Trembling legs unsure in their footing
Excruciating pain all but breaking my
    heart
Rivers of tears silently flowing
Will I ever again see my parents alive?

Brought to a place of new faces, new names
Where sandy-haired children were happy
    and playing
Hard to blend in with their fun and their
    games
Seeking to obscure my own dark features
Strangers around me unconfined and free
Reaping the harvest of crops and of hay
The ghetto so far yet so near to my heart
Mama had sent me ribbons for my hair
Which I kept hidden under my pillow
Clutching them at night I wet them with
    tears
Mama, papa, please take me back
Let's all die together, don't leave me here
    alone

And so it came to pass that the danger
    was over

And I could return to the ghetto again
The exhilarating joy of being together
Of hugging, and kissing and crying in
    glee
Blood rushing freely from my nose in
    excitement
A miracle of God for both child and
    parents
Reaffirming our faith as in biblical days
That God would spare us His chosen
    people
That Moses would lead us out of our
    bondage
So many more trials still to endure
So many more times coming so close to
    death
Perpetual survivors in a hopeless world
Vivid memories to collectively keep alive
To testify, to speak of
And to remember

A Silent Visit

(My father dying of Alzheimer's disease)

I come to visit you in your now silent
    world
Once vibrant beings now merely shadows
Wheel chairs moving down long alien
    corridors
Helpless people calling for a nurse
Oblivious to any life around them
I enter your room with a sense of anguish
Will I now find you totally departed?
I gaze into your deep brown eyes
Pupils magnified through your reading
    glasses
A smile of recognition at seeing me
My face still familiar in your short-
    circuited memory
Papa do you know me?
Do you still remember Mirele?
Mumbles and slurs of unrecognizable
    sounds
No longer able to recall the past
Of days of bravery and valor
Greatness now forever stilled, forever
    muted
Holocausts of horror
and glory of survival and of faith

Is this God's reward to a hero of the
    Jewish people?
The sunset to a full yet cruel life
You smile at David and at Sarah:
Havi's children, papa
Life and beauty alive and growing
Taking our places
It is their turn now
To experience and live life
I love you papa!

Hand in Hand

(My mother dying of cancer)

Shadows of leaves flickering in the
    moonlight
Desperate voices lost in total darkness
Sounds of snow crushing beneath our feet
Panic consuming our frozen bodies
Partisans refusing to give us refuge
"We implore you, take us with you
Don't leave us here to die
You have arms to protect you
We can keep up with your pace
I will carry my child and run"
Angry men pushing us away
"We do not want you helpless women"
Mama, mama what will happen to us
    now?

Run, run we have to follow them
Otherwise there is no hope
I cling to her, my mantle of protection
I am cold and hungry, mama
Be still Mirele, we have to run my child
My heart is beating in total fright
Where is papa, do these men know?
There my recollections end
I can't remember any more
Life's many ironies do repeat
You now clinging on to life
In a hospital all alone
Let me die with you mama
We can run again together
As we did that starry night

Judy

Together with the lilacs you too had
  flowered
Graced by the sun and the gentle rain
In your eyes were reflected the people
  who love you
Their memories of pain transformed into
  joy
A child of the Holocaust gave birth to a
  child
The legacy of a people was born within you
As I stand here beside you so many years
  later
Brimming with pride at my daughter
  beside me
The bearer of seeds that have ripened to
  fruit
Your eyes now reflect the children you
  bore
The magic of their essence was gifted to
  you
Now blessed anew with the coming of
  Hannah
The joy in your face when your arms
  embrace her
The reflection of her smile mirrored
  within you

As I sit here beside you on this *Yom Kippur*
Reciting the *Kaddish* for my own parents
I know that their essence is borne within us
That part of me also is alive within you
From Chana to Hannah the legacy continues
In our children we transcend the mortality of life
In their being our souls live on forever

The River of Life

(For my granddaughters Sarah and Hannah)

This river has its source in the high
mountain peaks
Where the snow-covered earth is touched
by the sun
Where embryonic fluid is spewing forth
life
Ripples and splashes of free-flowing love
Sustaining the flowers and trees on its
banks
Much as we do when we give birth to our
children
Nourishing their hearts and bodies with
love
Little ones born in our own image
Young lives unfolding as do flowers in
springtime
Caressed and held by loving embraces
Cradled in beauty
Unhindered and free
Ready to begin the adventure called life

Havi

Gemstone rivers from subterranean veins
Amethyst crystals once grounded in the
earth
Multifaceted mirrors and reflections of
time
So many different sides to living and
being
Energy surges from your heart and your
soul
Poured out as healing, caring and love
In your eyes one senses the depth of your
feelings
The awareness, perplexity and duality of
it all
Unanswered questions as to where you
are headed
Expressed in the songs and poems you
write
The loveliness of your voice bursting out
in laughter
So gentle and soft is your touch and
embrace
Your figures on canvas are touching and
loving
Sharing the flow and essence of life
The beauty and rhythm in all our tasks

The Zen of changing Sarah's wet diaper
Hearing David expressing his feelings
  this day
Choosing to be part of all life around us
Choosing to be apart and in touch with
  ourselves
A continuous search for meaning and
  substance
Ever growing, ever changing and
  discovering life
Love yourself, be yourself
You are beloved and special!

Tides to Reality

(My healing during psychotherapy)

Waves of anger battering the shore
Pounding the rocky boulders and earth
Eroding and stripping away the
    foundation
All that remains are last bits of sand
The hourglass is stripped of all of its
    grains
Face to face with my own self at last!
Hearing the music of the sounds of
    silence
Realizing the nature of my mission in life
Unhindered by fear of where I am headed
A passenger in a vehicle with freedom to
    travel
Hands on the steering wheel ready for
    changes
Choosing my own roads to the future
Aware of differences between reality and
    vision
Yet daring enough to pursue even dreams
Ever remembering my past of survival
Yet free and unhindered in the passages
    to come
Knowing where I've been
At peace where I am

The final awareness
That I have within me
Tools for discovery
A sense of adventure
To follow my dreams
To sing my own song
Comfortable at being alone
Unafraid of being different
Looking without for inspiration and
    guidance
Looking within for courage and faith
Experiencing life in all of its facets

Meditation

Envision the flow of a wandering river
Drift with its currents of ripples and rapids
Like water, so life, is ever moving and
    changing
Become one with the leaf that floats on
    its surface
Achieve liberation from life's limitations
Surrender to the beauty and divinity of its
    flow
Search out and express the creativity
    within you
Derive satisfaction from all that you do
Free up your mind from the constraints of
    your body
Become the master of what you choose to
    do
Seek your life's purpose without adding
    judgment
Emote inner feelings with candor and
    openness
Treat kindly and gently the people around
    you
Respect all their feelings and private
    inner spaces
Attune your senses to the ambience
    around you

Listen to the notes of the music of your
	soul
View the energies of colors and the
	essence of nature
Embrace those you love or those who
	need a hug
Smell the lilacs in spring and evergreens
	in winter
Bite into a juicy apple
Fly a kite on a breezy afternoon
Go ahead and hug a cloud
Alas, in your quest for the kernel of life's
	wisdom
Your only reward may be a bowl of
	popcorn
So munch on it and enjoy it
And be thankful for how delicious it
	tastes

The Silent Aleph א

Breathe deeply, inhale, the life force
  around you
Muffle all sounds of ambient distractions
Let go of your thoughts, your fears, and
  your pain
Loosen the restraints of your physical
  body
Surrender your being to the power of
  your mind
To the silent inner wisdom of your higher
  self
Envision reflections from transparent
  crystals
View the awesome and quiescent
  nothingness of space
Therein you will find God's
  omnipresence
And therein you will find the divinity
  within you
Messengers will address you through
  mystical letters
They will speak to you in tones of our
  ancient tongue
They'll reveal to you the meaning of the
  silent aleph א
The oneness אchad of אlohim our God

The multiplicity of all facets of the
  human experience
The zen and transcendence in all that we
  do
Creativity and intuition, courage and faith
In my quest to reach for the silent aleph א
Is the magnificent obsession to know the
  divine

Center Point Large Print
600 Brooks Road / PO Box 1
Thorndike ME 04986-0001 USA

(207) 568-3717

US & Canada:
1 800 929-9108
www.centerpointlargeprint.com